This IS the Day

This *IS* the Day

A Year of Observing Unofficial Holidays about
Ampersands, Bobbleheads, Buttons, Cousins,
Hairball Awareness, Humbugs, Serendipity,
Star Wars, Teenagers, Tenderness, Walking to
School, Yo-Yos, and More

Andrew Taylor-Troutman

RESOURCE *Publications* · Eugene, Oregon

THIS IS THE DAY
A Year of Observing Unofficial Holidays about Ampersands, Bobbleheads, Buttons, Cousins, Hairball Awareness, Humbugs, Serendipity, Star Wars, Teenagers, Tenderness, Walking to School, Yo-Yos, and More

Resource Publications
An Imprint of Wipf and Stock Publishers
199 W. 8th Ave., Suite 3
Eugene, OR 97401

www.wipfandstock.com

PAPERBACK ISBN: 979-8-3852-3388-5
HARDCOVER ISBN: 979-8-3852-3389-2
EBOOK ISBN: 979-8-3852-3390-8

VERSION NUMBER 11/25/24

To the congregation of Chapel in
the Pines Presbyterian Church

The truest words I ever heard about divine love were uttered once by a friend as a grace before a meal. He bowed his head, in the guttering candlelight, steam rising from the food before him, the fingers of the cedar outside brushing the window, and said, "We are part of a Mystery we do not understand, and we are grateful."

—Brian Doyle, "Joey's Doll's Other Arm"

Contents

Acknowledgments

I've NOTICED THAT MANY authors end this section by thanking their families, but I'd like to begin with gratitude for Ginny, who shares the days with me. We love our three children every single day, and they teach us about faith, hope, and love. Also, about Fortnite.

I learned how to write by mimicking writers whom I love, until I found my own voice in harmony with theirs. Brian Doyle once told me that we writers are "a big chortling inky clan." He was a huge influence. This project also riffs off the work of Ross Gay, especially his two collections of delights. Carson Brisson was my Hebrew professor, and he remains my greatest role model in writing, a person of faith with humility and humor.

I also learned from my colleagues in the doctoral program at Pittsburgh Theological Seminary. I'm grateful to all of you, including Scott and Andy, who are my mentors. Special thanks for specific help with this book to Molly, Porsha, Sarah, Taylor, and Walter (who wants to save the world). The six of us spent many days with teacher and author Melissa Butler. What a gift to be in her classes! Melissa is the best! ("Andrew," she said calmly, "You are a writer who uses a lot of exclamation points.")

I've dedicated this book to the congregation of Chapel in the Pines because every day is a gift to serve alongside of you. And let all God's people say, "Go Heels!"

Introduction: Why *This* Day?

"This is the day," I announce every Sunday from the front of the church, "that the Lord has made." The congregation responds with the second half of Psalm 118:24: "Let us rejoice and be glad in it."

Typing this refrain, I wonder how to punctuate the congregation's response. While spoken in unison, there are many inflections, tones, and emotions. More than a few folks join the chorus in monotone; maybe someone stifles a . . . yawn. Other folks are chipper, answering with a robust exclamation point! Some look a little puzzled, maybe because this is their first visit, or perhaps they are not sure if this day is actually something to rejoice and be glad about. Over the years, I've led this refrain hundreds of times. From week to week, whether I'm tired or bright-eyed, I say the same thing: "This is the day." What does that mean? What am I talking about?

To answer those questions, I want to step outside of the church. I want to take you into the wider community. I want to think about other days of the week.

Let me introduce you to a national day.

Actually, you've probably heard of one. Maybe you saw a restaurant promoting National Taco Day (October 4) or your local coffee shop celebrating National Cappuccino Day (November 8). There are over 1,500 unofficial holidays listed at NationalDayCalendar.com. There may be contradictions when a single calendar day encompasses multiple celebrations: February 21 is National Sticky Bun Day and National Grain-Free Day.

The following pages of this book do not discuss sticky buns or grain-free diets, but many other celebrations did intersect with my life in unusual, often revelatory ways, helping me to become more fully aware of what I have and who I interact with on a daily basis. I also became curious about exceptionally weird national days. What does hanging a slab of bacon in the foyer on National Flitch Day have to do with marital fidelity? I hope you'll keep reading.

~

This book is a yearlong journal of observing unofficial holidays for such things as ampersands, bobbleheads, buttons, cousins, hairball awareness, humbugs, serendipity, Star Wars, teenagers, tenderness, walking to school, Yo-Yos, and more. My experiences with these national days are told chronologically, and the stories within each month are divided into sections by a tilde (~).[1] My brother, John, a mathematician, taught me that this squiggly sign indicates similarity between objects. I also have in mind what my teacher, Melissa Butler, calls a feathered essay. I picture the sections and paragraphs as little birds in the air, which swoop and loop and maybe scuffle and tussle with one another, eventually landing, however precariously, on a point (or points).

I also hope readers will have fun!

However, this does not mean that I am unaware that serious, even tragic, realities make up many of our days. I began by asking you to imagine standing before a congregation every Sunday, aware of the various tones of the worshippers and some of the emotions behind their voices. To allude to the rock band R.E.M., not only shiny, happy people holding hands need to rejoice and be

---

1. You're someone who reads footnotes! Until I started reading Ross Gay, I rarely bothered with footnotes. Ross makes footnotes fun! Since you're here, I'll share a cool fact: the word tilde is derived from the Greek for "little horn." There is no National Tilde Day, but in addition to the citations, I promise to sprinkle in more fun footnotes in the pages to come. It'll be our little secret.

glad in the day. The most vivid Sundays in my memory are when I have seen tears in someone's eyes.

With colleagues in a doctoral program at Pittsburgh Theological Seminary, I spent two weeks with poet and essayist Ross Gay, who describes how joy is neither the absence nor the antithesis of sorrow. Ross asked, "What if joy is not only entangled with pain, suffering, or sorrow, but [joy] is also what emerges from how we care for each other *through* those things?"[2] My greatest hope for this book is to serve as a means for readers to discover this kind of entangled joy.

Why not start *this* day?

2. Gay, 8

January: Tender Repairs

I DECIDED TO ORDER a personalized bobblehead doll for my birthday. I couldn't justify the expense (over $150) except as a gift to myself. My wife, Ginny, was agreeable, if a little puzzled. She asked more than once, "Are you sure?" I kept nodding, like a bobblehead.

As per their design, bobbleheads nod agreeably. My kids are still at the age where they cry, "No!" to just about everything I suggest. Wouldn't it be a change to have someone around who regularly agrees with even my silly ideas?

There is a wider appeal for these unusual figures. January 7th is National Bobblehead Day. I read somewhere that Disney characters all have large heads compared to their bodies because we find it comforting. It makes them appear more childlike. It also allows oversized eyes and mouths, which communicate clear feelings. There is a time for nuance, but you don't want Mickey Mouse or your bobblehead to be cryptic or shrouded in mystery.

The company personalizes a bobblehead by modeling its face after mine. I sent photographs of my head from the front, back, and both sides. The manufacturer then provides a diverse selection of stock bodies, each capable of donning dozens of distinct outfits. I thought about some of the clergy outfits, but my desire for a bobblehead did not relate to my professional life. Other options included casual outfits, even writerly ones, such as posing with a journal or book in hand. My bobblehead body could have matched my hiking hobby.

I decided on a baseball uniform, specifically catcher's equipment—my position in high school.

The first bobbleheads were baseball players, a gimmick to draw fans to the stadium. But the allure for me was personal. I'm in my fourth decade now, and as I've grown, reflection on the new year has become more intertwined with awareness of passing time. Looking at my image in the catcher's gear reminds me of my youth. I've forgotten most of the wins and losses, the successes and failures. What remains are the smells of cut grass and leather gloves, the texture of dirt between my fingers and the bat in my hands, and the joy of a team sport, which is a timeless feeling of connection to something greater than one's self. This is healthy nostalgia, right?

My bobblehead definitely agrees with me.

～

My birthday coincides with National Word Nerd Day! When I excitedly broke this news to Ginny, she smiled and responded that this one was "in your wheelhouse."

Wheelhouse is such a wonderful word to nerd out on. I know it from baseball, where it refers to a batter's preference—a portion of the strike zone where a batter can hit a pitch with the most power. After a home run, an announcer might comment, "That pitch was in her wheelhouse."

Outside the ballpark, wheelhouse refers to any area of expertise and interest. Ginny is the Minister of Member Engagement at our church, meaning she interacts with a variety of age levels to help them feel welcomed and connected to the community of faith. She's perfect for this position.

A wheelhouse was originally defined as an enclosed area on a ship. At sea, challenges certainly arise, but a captain can navigate the ship to safety from the wheelhouse. It's a specialized position that demands skill.

There are lots of metaphors for sailing: smooth seas, choppy waters, dropping anchor. People often perceive life as a journey. As this experiential year unfolds, I'll enjoy some national days and dislike others. I will broaden my horizons.

~

Since Martin Luther King Jr. Day is on the third Monday of January, there are a wide range of unofficial holidays that, depending on the year, might fall on the same date, such as National Bagel Day, National Fig Newton Day, and National Hot Buttered Rum Day. Another day marks both National Penguin Day and National Disc Jockey Day. Yet another salutes famous people, whether fictional (like Popeye the Sailor and Winnie the Pooh) or larger than life (like the inimitable Betty White). Throughout this year, I'll have to make choices to exclude certain celebrations, but at other times, I might celebrate the various national holidays together.

MLK Jr. Day fell on January 19, which happens to be National Tenderness Toward Existence Day. I initially wondered if tenderness could be better celebrated in the spring, when many animals care for their broods. But as I drove home from a march and voter registration rally, I noticed tenderness in the leafless trees, their bare branches wiping away the cold, gray sky.

Beneath a tree in a playground, I spotted a burly man with tattoos adorning both arms, proudly carrying a gaudy unicorn backpack over his shoulder. I mean *gaudy,* sparkling rainbow sequins. He looked at his daughter in such a tender way. Tender the way.

Tender the way yet another grown child closed her hand over her mother's, reaching for the bill as if to say, "Let me get this." Tender the way a fellow dad texts me as Buddy—thanks, Greg. Tender the way the woman in the souped-up truck with enormous tires drove with a Jack Russell Terrier in her lap, the little dog's head sticking out the window, tongue flapping. Tender the way another dad in the park kicked the soccer ball so that his child could trap it. Tender the way a little guy placed wildflowers in his mom's hair. Tender the way she sat motionless in the grass, legs crisscrossed, back perfectly straight. Tender the way a grown son guided his elderly father by the elbow through an opened door and the way the older man allowed his son to lead.

When I slow down and look for tenderness, it is more accessible to me.

This time of year, people often quote Dr. King using the same lines.[1] But flipping through a collection of his sermons led me to one he preached in 1959, before the marches and rallies that made him famous. Riffing on a verse from Matthew ("Be ye therefore wise as serpents and harmless as doves"), King called for having "a tough mind and a tender heart."[2] Tenderness is not weakness. It takes a strong mind to resist evil. It takes a tender heart to resist with love.

∿

Cwtch is a Welsh word (not a misprint). Pronounced as "kutch," it rhymes with "dutch." The word originally referred to a small cupboard. Let's call it a cubby—that delightful word often on the lips of elementary schoolers in reference to their small, sacred space in the classroom. A cwtch is the kind of feeling that can make you feel like a kid again. To return to a cubby, a safe place. January 25 is a version of Valentine's Day in Wales that recognizes and celebrates the cwtch in all special relationships.

Today, I visited my younger son's second-grade classroom. I sat in a wooden chair with the class seated crisscross applesauce before me on a dark blue rug. My son had the place of honor right

---

1. My personal go-to line is King's reference to the "thingification" of human beings in his 1967 speech to the Southern Christian Leadership Conference. King critiqued American foreign policy, specifically the Vietnam War, by making a connection to the economic system of slavery: "A nation that will keep people in slavery for 244 years will thingify them and make them things. And therefore, they will exploit them and poor people generally and economically. It will have to use its military might to protect these interests. All these problems are tied together."

2. King, 47

next to me. I read a book about Mr. Putter and his cat, Tabby. It's a story about writing a list of good things: yellow cats, old sweaters, cinnamon toast, and long baths. I read slowly, making sure to pause to show the illustrations like my mom used to do, and the kids laughed in all the funny places.

When we finished, his teacher allowed my son to walk me to the head office. He told me that he was working on his own story about a dog named Lyman and a hamster named Peanut. "I love those names," I told him. "Will you read your story to me once it's finished?"

He gave me a long hug, which is very good and definitely at the top of my list.

~

January 28 was like any other day in that I stepped on a LEGO piece, causing that all-too-familiar pain to course through my foot. But it happened to be the anniversary of the patent submission for LEGO bricks in 1958.

The abbreviation of two Danish words, "leg godt," which means "play well," is the source of the name LEGO. (A lovely example of word-nerd trivia.) I also learned that LEGO produces 36,000 pieces per minute and sells seven sets globally every second. The volume of LEGO bricks sold in a single year would circle the globe five times. No wonder I keep stepping on them.

I appreciate that my kids enjoy LEGOs. It's fun to see them advance their skills by following the detailed directions and fitting tiny pieces together. Instead of swooping in to help, Ginny and I want to encourage and empower them. It's tough to watch them fail, yet with tenderness, we can help them learn to repair.

Despite the Batmobile's intended age for older children, our son persistently requested it. After we finally relented and bought it for him, he grew increasingly frustrated with the complex directions and small pieces. I managed to get him to bed that night, but he woke up ridiculously early to continue his project on his own. He came to our bedroom and asked for help, but I was too tired and stayed in bed. Several minutes later, I heard a crash. I found him crying at the kitchen table, with LEGOs littering the floor. He'd smashed the half-finished Batmobile on the floor in frustration.

As I crawled around on my hands and knees, picking up pieces, my bare knee came down hard on a LEGO, and a curse word escaped my mouth. My son, who had been watching from his seat at the table, looked at me in surprise. Then he grinned.

Smiling back, I asked, "Just what the hell is so funny?"

He burst into giggles. Wiping his eyes, he joined me on the floor, and together we put everything back in the box, then on his shelf beside other LEGOs.

Eventually, he and his brother used the Batmobile pieces to craft different vehicles of their own design, including a Batboat that he would run downstairs carrying, then swoop around the kitchen table. To this day, he'll look at me with a mischievous grin and say, "What the hell, Dad?"

February: Awesome Deliveries

February kicks off with National Ukulele Day. A couple of years ago, my wife gave me a ukulele when I turned forty years old, and this remains one of my all-time favorite gifts. I love to play, including saying "Happy Birthday" to other people.

I realize that not everyone appreciates the uke. But the only negative thing I can say about the instrument relates to the name itself: ukulele means "jumping fleas" in Hawaiian. Gross. This association aims to replicate the motion of the plucked strings, but let's find a comparison that doesn't bite. As the most famous ukulele song is "Somewhere Over the Rainbow" by Hawaiian native Israel "Iz" Kamakawiwoʻole, instead of "jumping fleas," let's rename the uke in memory of him—the Kamakawi. Has a ring to it!

The original uke makers were Portuguese immigrants who made a new instrument based on models from their homeland. This lineage dates all the way back to the kithara in the Old Testament, commonly known as a lyre. That ancient instrument was intended for beginners, including children, and small hands can still play the modern uke. There are only four strings instead of six or twelve on a guitar, and the frets are much closer together. Plus, you can play several chords by fingering only one string and strumming the rest.

My daughter received her own uke for her fourth birthday, and, while she hasn't quite mastered the "Happy Birthday" song, she strums her own tunes and sings her own lyrics. She com-posed a song, "Gimme Sunshine."

February doesn't readily call to mind sunshine, rainbows, or Hawaiian beaches. Despite having the fewest days, it can be a dreary, seemingly interminable month. February includes Ash Wednesday, when Christians mark their foreheads with ashes in the sign of the cross as a way to remember our mortality. Cold, damp, grim Febru-ary says, "You will die." Of course, that is true.

But the uke wants us to have fun![1] It's lovely to dedicate a day to the bright, ping-y sounds, which almost always lift my spirits, especially in a month when I need it most.

~

Postal workers likely prefer the eleven official holidays that give them a day off work. However, even though it is unofficial, Febru-ary 4 is still a day to thank the person who delivers your mail.

The term "snail mail" betrays the bias of the digital age with its rapid downloads and lightning-fast streaming, not to mention email. Oh, email. On certain days, an overwhelming number of reply-all messages plague my professional life. "Go postal" means to erupt in anger from stress. I'm not a Luddite, yet technological advancement in the name of efficiency often comes at the expense of personal connection.

Over the years, I've known several mail carriers. At my small, liberal arts school, each student had a tiny mailbox in the student center. If a package was too big to fit, a slip of paper instructed you to go downstairs to the mailroom. As a freshman, I happened to tell the mail carrier that the box was from my mom. I was feel-ing homesick that day, and it must have shown. For the rest of my college career, Nancy drew a little smiley face on the slip of paper before sliding it into my mailbox.

---

1. You will have noticed by now that, in my writing, I am a big fan of the exclamation point! I have tried to be judicious in my use of this particular punctuation mark (thanks to my readers, especially Melissa Butler, for your help). But I also have a lot of fun!

I was also friendly with the two mailmen in seminary. When Ginny and I married and moved into a small townhome, our letters were delivered through the slot in the front door. And our dog, Nikki Giovanni (named in homage to the poet), would bite the mail as it dropped into the house. (Not very writerly of her.) My study desk faced the street, and I could see when our mail carrier would park on the street, then carry the mail in her satchel to hand deliver to all the townhomes. To keep teeth marks off my correspondence, I'd greet her outside. Her name was Bernice. On hot days, I'd give her a bottle of water, and we would talk under the shade of an oak tree. Bernice grew up in Richmond, and she told me that, as a Black child, she never would have walked alone in this part of town. She had a habit of saying, "Lord, in mercy fathom," whenever something was hard to believe or outrageous.

I'm on friendly terms with our current mail carrier. Her name is Rhonda. A year or so ago, she left a polite but serious note for the kids to stop putting leaves and pine cones inside our mailbox. Now, my kids leave chalk drawings on the sidewalk for Rhonda to enjoy.

One of my neighbors, Barb, works for a certain delivery company that requires her to dress in silly short brown pants. She laughs at how her work uniform "shows off my legs." I see her around town, most recently outside our co-op. She ran over to me for a hug and grinned, "Andrew, we get to serve and help other people. How awesome it that?!"

∾

My kids are preacher's kids—actually, double preacher's kids, because both their mom and I are in ministry. On February 8, we recognize the odd and wondrous life of a preacher's kid.

On Sunday morning, I'm anxious to get my kids out the door. They make every excuse to stay home. Just recently, after squalling for several minutes that I didn't have to waste, I relented when the middle child laid down a bargaining chip—he would get dressed if he could play his choice of music. He picked up the tablet while I gathered my papers into my briefcase.

Then the air filled with the unmistakable opening guitar riff of Nirvana's "Smells Like Teen Spirit."

Lord, in mercy fathom!

The screaming vocals of the troubled, beautiful genius Kurt Cobain brought to mind my own adolescence when I, too, protested going to church. We had to take some time for holy headbanging.

~

I'm writing before a group of elementary school students at recess, four of whom have mullet haircuts.

There are eighty species of mullet (the fish) and almost as many names for the hairstyle: the coat rack, 10-90, Camaro crash helmet, hockey hair, beaver paddle, Tennessee top hat, Mississippi mud flap, and achy breaky big mistakey. Although Mike D of the Beastie Boys popularized the term in his 1994 song "Mullet Head," artifacts dating back to first-century Great Britain show evidence of the haircut. The cut was useful for keeping the hair out of the eyes and the neck warm, according to one scholarly theory. Perhaps this is what appeals to modern third-graders. I noticed that, unlike their classmates on this cold February day, these mullet heads did not wear caps or hoods.

Or maybe they just showed off their style. Business in the front, and party in the back.

These children may be copying the preferences of their older siblings, cousins, and neighbors. According to the website Beauty Launchpad, Gen-Z is "the most obsessed with this shaggy style." There are Instagram pages to prove this claim.

I, a late Gen-Xer, keep my hair short all the way around, both for convenience and for social acceptability. At this stage in my life, I'm not looking to make waves with a so-called Kentucky waterfall.

Yet, I admire these children running free, as unrestrained as their long hair flying behind them.

～

There are actually two days in February when you can eat ice cream for breakfast. But before I mention those national days, the thought strikes me that, in theory, one could eat ice cream any day, even every day for breakfast. That being said, doing something unusual seems like a good excuse to look for national holidays. Changing your routine might just change your perspective.

The celebration on February 18 is not to be confused with Ice Cream for Breakfast Day on the first Saturday in February. That holiday dates back to 1966 in Rochester, New York, when Florence Rappaport, a social worker and mother of six children, offered the frozen treat for breakfast as a way to appease her restless and grumpy brood, who were stuck inside due to a snowstorm. As they grew up and traveled, her kids took the observance around the world. Recently, the largest celebrations have been in Jerusalem.

National Eat Ice Cream for Breakfast Day has a vastly different origin story. February 18 was the birthday of Malia Grace, a nine-year-old who died of cancer in 2010. A few years later, close family friends remembered her life with the special treat she loved. The holiday has grown as a way to remember the dead and support other children with cancer.

In my career as a pastor, I've visited many children's hospitals. I have met kids around Malia Grace's age and even younger who were very sick. On some level, ignorance is bliss. Many caregivers try to shield their young ones from the harsher realities of life, including death. Children with cancer don't have that option.

Yet, I have witnessed certain children wear hope and faith, as apparent to me as their hospital gowns decorated with zoo animals. They delight in the smallest things, like balloons, cookies, or ice cream. Every visitor is special and lights up their face with a smile.

My seminary professor and mentor, Carson Brisson, used to say, "I don't think our job in the ministry is to say how deep something is or how long it will be until dawn. We say, "I come in the name of someone who will stand with you through the

11

deep and dark." The name will vary depending on the individual and their faith. Maybe it's Jesus, Allah, the universe, or Taylor Swift. Whatever name brings hope and comfort; whatever food or music brings joy and delight; we share whatever life-giving we can find amid tragedy.

In other words, gimme sunshine and gimme ice cream.

I know of a child who has suffered five cancer relapses in three years. Today, I ate ice cream for breakfast and remembered him. My preacher's kids were all on board with this way of praying.

~

The PTA has a sign at the entrance to my children's elementary school. Occasionally, they crack dad jokes, such as, "What is red and smells like blue paint?" Red paint!

Today, the sign informed us that, this spring, over one trillion cicadas will emerge from the ground. This is the most since 1803. My first thought is that there should be a national day for this.

My kindergartener felt sorry for the scientists who had to collect this data. Counting one trillion of anything would be tiresome. But especially bugs. You might lose your mind, if not your religion.

I wonder what our early nineteenth-century friends thought of their cicada eruption. America was experiencing the Second Great Awakening, a Protestant religious revival characterized by fire and brimstone preaching. Perhaps they believed cicadas to be a sign of the apocalypse.

A fellow parent told me, "You can start your day over anytime you want," while we were waiting for our kids after school. This statement struck me as a way to live in the moment, a philosophy that many prophets, sages, and mystics have preached over the years.

But if I had to count cicadas, I wouldn't want to start over.

I might argue that the essential religious truths are universal. We teach them to our kindergarteners, along with their numbers and letters. Share what you have. Do unto others as you would have them do unto you. Raise your hand to go to the bathroom.

Do cicadas have their own religions? Maybe they follow the Golden Rule: treat other cicadas as you would like to be treated. I know from my youth that, lying in the cool grass on a warm night, with the stars shimmering in the sky above, the sound of cicadas felt like worship. There are moments in life that we cannot categorize or quantify. There are some things that are too large or enormous to count. We only know enough to be in awe of what is greater than us, our ability to comprehend, and, if we are lucky, we hold our loved ones close.

~

I started writing to a new person this year. He is in jail. I think again of Carson, my former seminary professor, saying, "I don't think our job in the ministry is to say how deep something is or how long it will be until dawn."

In my letters, I ask about his basic needs, like food and health. I also express my hope for his mental wellbeing. He is a praying person, so I wrote a prayer for him: *Lord of the night and day, the twilight, the fiery dawn, and all times between, help us to believe where we have not seen, to trust we are not alone, and to have your grace carry us home.*

Many postal workers, including a mail carrier for this prison, were involved in delivering my letter to him. I rely on numerous individuals, most of whom I'll likely never meet, to deliver his reply. He reported that he is safe and doing the best he can to keep his hopes up. The other day, he caught a glimpse of a deer through the security bars of the outdoor compound. Thanks to his letter, I don't look at deer the same way.

March: Awkward Laughs

AT DARK THIRTY, I slipped out of bed and crept downstairs. After doing some yoga to the tune of the coffee percolator, I leashed our house coyote and opened the door just as a group of ten teenagers strolled up the middle of the neighborhood street. Not wanting the dog to bark, I froze in the doorway. But there was something else that anchored me in the shadows: sympathy. I didn't want to embarrass them. Also, I didn't want to know if they were getting into trouble. I wanted to let them be.

National Teenager Day (March 21) has brought them to mind again. Brian Doyle wrote a poem about finding a dead sparrow, which he realized must have been the bird equivalent to a teenager. "We get so impatient with teenagers," he notes. "We want them to leap past stupid. But stupid is a great teacher, isn't it?"[1]

From my own stupid behavior, I learned a great many things: not to leap into the bed of a moving pickup truck; not to drive your friend's two-door Mazda through a muddy field; not to have a competition to eat the most burritos from Taco Bell; not to sneak out at night by climbing from your bedroom window into the pricker bush below, thereby letting out a shriek that will wake your mother; not to skip a history test, then show up at the basketball game in which your history teacher happens to double as the assistant

1. Doyle, 106

coach. I also learned not to paint letters on your chest to show off at football games if the forecast is below freezing.[2]

I don't know what those teenagers were doing walking the neighborhood in the wee hours of the morning. I am a middle-aged person who uses phrases like "wee hours" in my writing. (Lord, in mercy fathom.) All I know is that, from the doorway, I experienced the boldness of their long-legged tribe. They paraded down the middle of the street like they owned it, which, at that moment, they did. They were beautiful in the moonlight.

The tallest dude saw me and broke the spell with a wave of his hand: "Good evening." There was a peal of laughter. "It's morning," a girl replied. As they continued to stroll, she added, "You're such an ass."

⌒〜

A young Swiss accordion player named Werner Thomas composed "Der Ententanz" in the late 1950s. This "Duck Dance" became a big hit at the local resort, but it likely would have stayed there if not for a Belgian producer who brought the tune to America. By the late 1980s, "The Chicken Dance" had become a cultural phenomenon. Following that, March 14 was declared a national day.

Minor league baseball games evoke my memories of the song and dance. I remember flapping my arms with gusto as a young boy, then rolling my eyes as an adolescent. I enthusiastically participate now; it's like a dad joke—corny fun.

There are five years between my oldest and my youngest, which increasingly feels like a chasm. At eleven years old, my first-born is embarrassed by the Chicken Dance and any public display of silliness, such as his "baby" sister vigorously flailing her arms and shaking her tail. I get it. I remember.

---

2. My adventure, however, falls short of my younger brother's. He had a classmate who was a major college basketball prospect, so popular that ESPN came to film one of the high school home games. My brother and his four friends each painted one letter on their chests: E-S-P-N-! Next, they rearranged their positions to spell P-E-N-!-S.

But there's also something beautiful about abandoning yourself to a silly moment. Consider freeing yourself to dance. I remember a poem by poet Rosemerry Wahtola Trommer: "My heart wheeled and my senses stretched out—and I couldn't stay clenched. I couldn't. Not that some part of me didn't try."[3] This poem feels like a prayer for a teenager. For my son.

~

March 19 is National Let's Laugh Day, which is fittingly celebrated on heels—I mean the tail feathers of the Chicken Dance. Not to be confused with International Moment of Laughter Day (April 14) or World Laughter Day (first Sunday of May), National Let's Laugh Day caught my attention due to its implied infectiousness—let's laugh together. You and me. "All y'all," as we say down South. I am grateful to catch something positive, especially in light of the plethora of diseases that my children bring home from the petri dish that is their school.

So, I thought I'd celebrate with a list of people whose delightful laughs, in turn, cause me to join them, even if I'm not feeling my best.

Matt works at the local co-op grocery store. The registers are close to the produce section, and I love it when my bushy-bearded friend's surprisingly high-pitched, sweet peal of laughter reaches my ears as I peruse the blueberries and cherries.

My paternal grandfather, Ray, died in 2011. Part of the sadness of his death is that he never met my kids. He would have been a wonderful great-grandfather—the corny king of knock-knock jokes. His belly laugh has not faded from my memory. Nor his silliness at singing all three words to "O Christmas Tree" over and over. I taught this to my children when they were very young, and I hope this tradition continues into the eye-rolling teenage years.

---

3. Trommer writes and publishes a daily poem on her website, *A Hundred Falling Veils* (ahundredfaillingveils.com). I remember this one, in particular, because it was published on my birthday (January 9).

A woman at my church named Susie starts laughing in the middle of her story, and though she hasn't yet narrated the humorous part, I can't help but crack up with her.

My firstborn, my preteen, snorts when he laughs. There is nothing more delightful in my world. Though he's increasingly conscious of how people perceive him in public (as well as his goofy father), every now and then, he'll cut loose a snort, which makes me thrilled to experience a moment of unrestrained joy with him.

On my desk at church is a framed photo of me reading to our three kids in our daughter's bed one Saturday morning. I was reading one of Mo Willems's Pigeon books (in a silly voice, of course) when Ginny just happened to walk into the room. She snapped a picture of all four of us in mid-laugh—mouths wide, eyes squinting. The picture is audible; I can hear us guffawing.

There are many conversations in my office that are serious, and more than a few are tearjerkers. Yet, sometimes, when I am alone, meditating, praying, or cursing about the awful unfairness of a particular suffering situation, I might glance at that picture. I might smile or even laugh out loud.

As someone who has been around many hospice and hospital rooms, I can tell you that laughter is often present in times of tragedy, even death. Perhaps this is due to the fact that our hearts are so open. We cannot stay clenched. A friend recently said that she had so much love for her child that it kept leaking out of her eyes in tears and spilling out of her mouth in laughter. I felt a stab of pain, then laughed in recognition.

Ginny and I were struggling to conceive a child when my parents took us, along with my brother and sister-in-law (Kelly), on a trip to Scotland as part of my father's sabbatical. Ginny and I wrestled with the heartache and frustration that would eventually lead us to seek fertility treatment even as we hiked the beautiful, rolling hills of the Outer Hebrides Islands. During one particularly long walk, a heavy rain chilled us to the bone. When we returned to the van, Ginny, Kelly, and Mom hung wool socks over their ears, pretending to be elephants. We all laughed until tears ran down our faces.

~

March 26 is Make Up Your Own Holiday. Here is my list.

Celebrate the National Day of Memorizing a Mary Oliver Poem, the National Day of Installing Rain Barrels, and the National Speech Pathologist Day (which, incidentally, already falls on May 18); National Day of Recipe for Magic; National Day to Yell at Car Radio Upon Hearing Report that Banks Are Reaping Profits For Said Profits Are on the Backs of Working People; National Day to Strike a Tree Pose in the Middle of Wooded Trail; National Day to Delight in Planning Halloween Costumes a Full Seven Months in Advance; National Day to Read Your Favorite Portion of *To Kill a Mockingbird*; National Day to Have Tea with Your Best Friend; National Day to Plan Your Next Great Adventure (Like Scuba Diving); National Day to Thank the Person Who Lets You Borrow Her Pickup Truck; National Day to Host a Vegetarian for Dinner; National Day to Look Courageously at One's Family System, Especially the Dysfunction; National Day to Remind Your Loved Ones That It Is Holy to Know What You Want; National Day to Read Your Son a Story Under a Tree in the Churchyard in Faith that One Day That Child Will Do the Same to His Own Kids.

All of these days are inspired by the habits, sayings, and initiatives of my mom, Anna, because March 26 is the day she was born. Happy birthday, Mom!

~

My friend, Jonathan, texted, "You're a pimple parent—congrats!" He was referring to the news of a small zit on the tip of my eleven-year-old's nose. Ginny had noticed this blemish while seated next to our firstborn at a restaurant. I remembered the first time that she and I took him out to eat at the very same establishment. He was still nursing, and he smooshed a greater amount of food onto his face than into his mouth. Now he's an adolescent, a tween with a zit on his nose. His little sister promptly declared that he looked like Rudolph.

Ginny later confided that she felt as sentimental as when our son lost his first tooth. There are no pimple fairies. Maybe I should give my son a dollar, but if his complexion is like mine, this might dip into the savings for braces.

There are no whimsical magical rituals to commemorate the onset of puberty. A national day for this?

"By the time I was eleven," wrote Richard Siken in *The New Yorker*, "I stopped being sad and started to be afraid."[4] Adolescence marks such a transition for many people. My grandfather, one of my heroes, died when I was that age. I started to be afraid, and that fear grew with me.

I worry about all my children. They will spend their entire school career training in case an armed intruder were to enter their classroom. They are already aware of wars overseas and police violence in our country. They know about the climate catastrophe. I will protect them as much as I am able. But that's the real fear: I am able to do precious little. The only certainties in life are death and pimples.

Long ago, a wry rabbi said, "Do not worry about tomorrow, for tomorrow will worry about itself." I don't think that is a call to put one's head in the sand. But I am a pimple parent. Why not accept people's congratulations? Why not celebrate the passage of time with each and every transition into maturity?

Despite my feelings of sentimentality and trepidation, I am proud of my son. For instance, when his little sister teased him about being Rudolph, he merely chuckled. Why not find humor when you can?

∾

My oldest son was beyond ready to leave, but I wanted a moment. I got down on one knee just by the door, like I used to do when

---

4. Siken, "Piano Lesson." *The New Yorker:* January 8, 2024

he was smaller. He's eleven years old now, and I look up at him from this vantage point.

"I'm proud of you for trying a new thing," I said.

After the door closed behind him, I went upstairs to write. I kept seeing him before me. Should I have said more? *Remember to breathe through your mouth, not your nose. If you don't get it right away, keep trying. Listen to your Nana; she knows best.*

But he already knew these things. Especially the last one.

When Mom turned sixty, she learned to scuba. She was pleased that my father had accompanied her. But her real designs were on her then-three-year-old grandson: "Don't you think he would like to have an adventure with me? Maybe when he's eleven."

When they returned from the pool, there was pride chiseled all over his face. Mom let him run ahead of her to me. She knows best. As I walked beside him back to the house, he reached for my hand. He had also reached out to me after his first day of kindergarten, and I had wondered if we would ever do so in the same way again.

April: Poetic Delights

APRIL IS NATIONAL POETRY Month, and this morning, I saw two goldfish crackers in the dirt outside my daughter's kindergarten classroom, apparently dropped by a child's little hands or maybe a parent trying to carry too much. Perhaps the crackers had spilled from a baggie. The fish had landed with their smiles shining in the sunlight, as if they were hiding a secret or something mysterious that most people would overlook on their way somewhere else. It struck me as poetic.

Mary Oliver said that she didn't know how to pray, but she knew how to pay attention, walk slowly, and kneel down in the grass.[1] She might not have had goldfish crackers in mind, but on April 1, I was grateful to see them. No fools.

My kids get super excited about April Fool's Day. But they will not out-prank their mom. One year, she ambushed them with silly string right when they walked in the door from school. Another year, she served a breakfast of "blood" pancakes (she had baked red beets into the batter).

Our kids have been scheming since February, and, thanks to the oldest one's computer skills, they have YouTube for inspiration.

---

1. Riffing on Oliver's famous poem, "The Summer Day," which you may know by the line, "What is it you plan to do with your one wild and precious life?" That's a prayer to me.

I sit back and watch. I'm happy to play along as the "victim" of someone's prank. I may even be genuinely fooled. For a brief moment, I believed those pancakes truly resembled blood. One of the greatest delights of my life is seeing my loved ones laugh.

~

Religious holidays have myths that accompany them, and I'm finding the same to be true for national days. April 7 is National Beer Day, and the myths about drinking alcohol, so often glorified in popular culture, are that booze makes you happier, looser, and hipper.

During the COVID-19 pandemic, Ginny and I were trying to juggle ministry and three kids living in our house. I developed the habit of cracking open a cold one at 5 p.m. I rationalized this as my way to relax. As the pandemic wore on, I found myself checking my watch more frequently and, sometimes, going to the fridge early. One beer became two, sometimes three.

The kids were often handling the stress in healthier ways. Our oldest was in school on Zoom. His teachers did the best they could under the circumstances, encouraging the students to pursue their own interests. He began to work on a graphic novel. His younger brother followed his lead, and he even helped him write the dialogue.

We created our own national day: Kid Author Day. I was unaware that April 10th is National Encourage a Young Writer Day. Ginny created an awesome banner to hang in our living room. In addition to their graphic novels, the boys made a stage out of cardboard boxes.

Friday is supposed to be my day off and devoted to my family. But I took several Zoom calls that afternoon. At the last minute, I ran out to the grocery store for a bottle of sparkling apple juice, which that morning I had promised Ginny that I would pick up. While at the store, I also decided to buy champagne. When I arrived home, I was already late for the scheduled reading. I popped the corks and guzzled a glass. Then another.

Throughout the event, our youngest daughter whined and wanted me to read her a book. She felt left out, and I tried to balance listening to the boys with giving attention to her. My head spun from the bubbly. No kid touched what my daughter called "sparky" apple juice. When I burned the frozen pizzas, I downed the rest of the champagne bottle.

Kid Author Day was not a total disaster. The boys read, and we clapped for them. After we choked down some burnt pizza, we escaped the smell of burnt crust by going outside, and the kids all ran ahead to the pond. As the evening sun sparkled on the water, I smiled at my wife.

Ginny frowned. "What's wrong with you?"

I tried to shrug her off. She persisted, "You seem so anxious."

I could have written this book solely about the national days devoted to drinks. Start on January 1 with National Bloody Mary Day and continue through National Champagne Day on December 31, observing celebrations for sangria, mint juleps, Indian Pale Ales, and buttered rum. Kate Richards, the creator of Instagram-famous cocktails made from ingredients in her garden, founded "Drinking with Chickens Day" on May 23.

April 7 marks National Beer Day because, in 1933, the Cullen-Harrison Act became law, ending the 13-year prohibition of this alcoholic beverage. With the rise in underground alcohol sales and subsequent mob violence, I think it is clear that making alcohol illegal was not an effective public health policy.

But alcohol is a depressant. And it is addictive—not for just a few people, but for everyone.

When I was drinking during the pandemic, I wasn't hungover every morning. I didn't lose my job. Neither drunk driving nor losing custody of my children led to my arrest. These are the "rock bottom" stories that often define alcoholism. In *The Naked Mind: Control Alcohol*, Annie Grace defines addiction as "having two competing priorities, wanting to do more and less of something at the same time."[2] Rationally, I could tell that I was drinking too often; I kept doing it, making various excuses.

2. Grace, 9

Grace continues, "You drink to get the feeling of peace that someone who is not dependent on alcohol always feels."[3] I want a deep peace that I can tap into even in times of stress, whether from work or family responsibilities, or even in the midst of a global crisis. Drinking will not help me find what I'm looking for.

Occasionally, I will have a beer with family or friends. But I'm also intentional about periods of abstaining. National Beer Day often falls within the Christian season of Lent, the forty days before Easter. For this period of time, it is common for people to fast or give something up, like caffeine or chocolate. The spiritual goal of fasting is not to deny yourself as a form of punishment but rather to give yourself space and make time for something else. Something like Grace's "feeling of peace." By fasting from alcohol not only in Lent but other months in the year, I have found that I now enjoy a beer on my own terms.

All three of my kids are now in school—no more Zoom! Though she has only started to read and write, the youngest also creates comics. I've suggested having another Kid Author Day, but there have been no takers so far. I lament that my drinking diminished the delight that day.

～

Lent can also involve adding something. You could substitute activities such as scrolling through your phone with prayer. My mom often memorizes a poem. The point is not for show but rather for your own wellbeing and, possibly, your relationship with God.

This year, I'm going to spend a few minutes every day standing barefoot outside. My family has a backyard the size of a postage stamp. The kids and the house coyote—that is, the dog—are harsh on the grass, leaving the majority of the yard covered in mud.

But there is a lovely patch of clover in the back corner. When the dog is inside, this is the local rabbits' munching ground. I believe the bunnies will be able to wait a short period of time while I stand barefoot in the clover. I want to add a small ritual that,

3. Ibid., 12

24

literally and metaphorically, grounds me in the world of dirt and growing things. I anchor myself momentarily in my physical form.

Ross Gay's poem "Thank You" inspired my idea for this: "Curl your toes into the grass ... Say only, thank you."[4]

This morning was bitterly cold. But as I stepped away from the soft carpet of clover, I admired how the tiny stalks popped back, relieved of my weight. For those with ears to hear, the clover whispers, "You're welcome."

~

My favorite cat belongs to one of our friends. This orange tabby bolts upstairs the moment my three rambunctious kids arrive and stays out of sight for our entire visit.

My future father-in-law once told his daughter not to trust a man who didn't like cats, so I damn well tried. Even so, I'm not exactly a cat person.[5] I won't be attending Hug Your Cat Day on June 4, much less "Happy Mew Year" on January 2 (a day for cats to celebrate the "mewness" of the year).

My wife's best friend from college taught her cat how to sit— in Spanish. Most cats follow their own rules, if not demands. The saying goes that dogs have masters and cats have servants.

On the other hand, cats seem easier to own than other pets. My brother knew people living in tiny New York City apartments who trained their cats to use the toilet, which must have been quite the party trick. Even cleaning the litter box seems more appealing than walking the dog outside in the rain, particularly when she takes her time. You can leave a cat alone for the weekend while you go on vacation. I suspect some cats may not even notice you've left.

Cats also bathe themselves; this is the reason for National Hairball Awareness Day on the last Friday in April. Cats need regular brushing to remove loose hair and prevent hairball regurgitation

4. Gay, *Against Which*

5. No disrespect to you, if you are a cat person. A former parishioner, Richard Guthrie, used to say, "You have the right to be wrong."

on your pillow. It seems like something a cat owner might wish to avoid. But a holiday to celebrate it? Probably a cat's idea.

However, the ancient and widespread spiritual teaching that you should love your neighbor as you love yourself reminds me that you must first love yourself. Cats don't seem to have a problem with this. I could use the reminder.

Ginny would like me to tackle my mad scientist eyebrows more often. I should attend to my hair and skin, as well as my clothes. Self-care is not self-absorbed or selfish.

Yet, Ginny also shared an episode of Dr. Becky's parenting podcast, *Good Inside*, featuring an interview with Pooja Lakshmin, the author of *Real Self-Care*. What I learned is that we often add self-care to our "should" or "must" list. If we are tired or weary, this can actually be self-defeating.

So, this odd holiday, National Hairball Awareness Day in April, has prompted me to think of self-love as not a chore or duty but a gift. Maybe I will hug a cat.

⤳

So, about self-care: I was past due for a haircut.

I sat down on one of the couches in the salon to wait. I thought about pulling out my iPhone, but there on the coffee table was an open box of Scrabble. I randomly scooped up six letters and looked at them. L-A-N-D popped to mind. However, I could use the other two letters to spell U-N-D-I-A-L. While I debated if "undial" was indeed a word, the door swung open and a father walked in with his young son. They sat in chairs across the table from me. Dad reached into his pocket and pulled out his iPhone, punched the code, and handed it over. The screen's glow immediately lit up the boy's face. He started to drool. No, it wasn't that bad.

I've certainly had times when I just needed to keep my child entertained while doing something in a public place. I'm not passing judgment on either the parent or the child. It is difficult enough for me to unplug (undial?) from my electronics. I returned my six letters.

Then I heard an audible kiss. The father had planted one on his son's cheek. And the child put down the phone. Of course, he promptly went back to it. But I was witness to that moment, right after that kiss, when father and son smiled at each other. Tender the way.

～

How do we find meaning in life when we are only here for a fleeting moment, and time rolls on like a river?

April 17 is National Haiku Day. About once a month during my first year of seminary, my friend Doug and I would agree to spend the whole meal talking only in haikus. Sentences with exactly seventeen syllables. We didn't plan this in advance, but rather when the mood struck us.

I am a planner. I like a schedule. I was a successful graduate student, in part because I appreciated the structure of a syllabus, which mapped out the coming term in clear assignments. Doug was also well organized, and he had a playful streak that was good for both of us. During those haiku-only lunches, we counted the syllables on our fingers as we spoke. For all the time and energy that I put into my academics, I can more easily recall bouncing haikus off Doug, collapsing with laughter in that little cafeteria.

This is not to suggest that the simple, three-line poetic form cannot communicate gravitas. Academics commonly recognize Kobayashi Issa (1763–1828) as one of the Japanese haiku masters. I've memorized Jane Hirschfield's translation of his poem so that I can carry it around with me.

On a branch
floating downriver—
a cricket, singing

Such a scene happens all the time, so part of Issa's art is to focus attention upon the extraordinary within the ordinary. What moves me most about this haiku is the ambiguity, which is achieved by painting a clear scene and leaving the interpretation

27

up to the reader. Is singing just what crickets do? Or is this cricket afraid? Does it sing knowing that drowning and death are likely a possibility? Is it a call for help? Might the cricket even be having fun on its ride?

Hirschfield interprets Issa with Zen Buddhism singing in the background; the river represents the impermanence of all life.[6] Such ideas flow through many religions, including my own. When the author of Ecclesiastes wrote that "all is vanity," he meant that nothing lasts. Since everything dies, how do we live today?

in my child's bed

his cold feet between my calves.

I am kept awake.

My poem is technically a senryu, which is similar to haiku in form. But instead of a haiku's focus on nature, senryu explores human emotions. I have tried to play with ambiguity in a simple scene. Cold feet keep a parent awake, but is that necessarily a problem? Might a father enjoy those late-night snuggles, thankful to be attentive to the moment?

∼

Back to my haircut. As I sat in the chair, I engaged my new hair-stylist in a conversation about other people's feet.

Over the years, the salon has expanded into the building next door, as well as opening a spa. Since it was much harder to get an appointment, I signed up with the newest employee. As she snipped away, I asked if she also worked in the spa. She explained that she had enough business cutting hair to pay her bills, but in her previous job, she had done pedicures. I replied that it must be "interesting" to work on other people's feet.

"You really get to know someone," she chuckled. Then she explained how many of her former clients were elderly and couldn't reach their own toenails. The nails would grow thick,

6. Hirschfield, 89

and as she clipped them, pieces would fly into her hair—once into her mouth! Lord, in mercy fathom!

As a pastor, I work with many elderly folks. But no toenails. The truth is that I'm squeamish about footwashing, although it is a Christian ritual often celebrated on Maundy Thursday, a few days before Easter.

But I recognize the importance of foot care and, even more, the gift of paying kind attention to someone. I told her that I thought what she did for those people was beautiful.

She shared that she still drives back over three hours roundtrip to give home pedicures to her former clients. This seemed Christ-like to me. On April 25, I celebrated National Hairdresser Appreciation Day by giving my new hairstylist a generous tip.

~

In honor of National Poetry Month, it seems fitting to close with one of my own poems.

A Still Small Voice

The kids wanted to prank their mom
on April Fools, and so we drove from
store to store, looking for silly string.
A veteran cashier sighed, "Yeah, well,
we used to carry it. Lord, what a mess."
This seemed a good lesson, how one
person's prank is another's chore,
empathy being the goal and humility
the final frontier. But the kids had their
hearts set, so we stopped at one more
and, just their luck, found cans on the shelf.
The prank went well, their mom being
a good sport, yet I shall remember most
the youngest saying, quietly to herself,
"I wished so hard, and it came true."

May: Beautiful Nonsense

OUR FAMILY VACATIONS AT the beach in early May, when it is still off-season. The little birds chirp on the deck as the sky rims red at dawn. The day unfolds with soft, small graces. There are joyous shrieks as my children race from the breaking ocean waves, followed by nose kisses under the towels and dribbles of popsicles down our chins. These are the moments so precious that I grieve their loss in the same instant they are happening. Love, like the ocean, is too vast for me to wrap my head around. I can only join my family in dancing on the beach after supper.

∾

May the Fourth be with you!

On this date, Star Wars fans around the world gather to watch movies, play video games, and eat cookies in the shape of Yoda. People dress up as characters and talk in their accents. I have a T-shirt with a picture of a certain green guy, wrinkled with age, and the words "Yoda Best Dad Ever." On any day of the year, I enjoy a pun.

The Christian greeting, "May the Lord be with you," may have inspired the famous Star Wars catchphrase, "May the Force be with you." George Lucas, the revered filmmaker, has described himself as a Methodist Buddhist, a nod toward the faith of his childhood and his adult exploration of another religion. It seems to me that the Jedi exhibit certain Buddhist principles such as mindfulness, compassion, and a belief in the interdependence of all things. Yoda can sound like a Zen teacher: "Attachment leads to jealousy. The shadow of greed, that is."

To quote Yoda once again: "My ally is the Force, and a powerful ally it is. Its energy surrounds us and binds us." Many religions regard this "it" as animating, life-giving, and gracious love. At the same time, the uniqueness of each individual faith is important. This is not to assert that one faith is superior to another—"judge not," as another Zen-like teacher once said—but to illustrate the abstract through the particular, such as a story of a tradition or culture.

When I was picking up my children from school, a fellow parent saw my Yoda Dad shirt and launched into an impersonation of some obscure character, assuming he and I were on the same page. Confused, I was. Still, it was fun to listen to him. One can learn a lot from a devotee of another faith tradition.

Finally, our kids ran over to us. They were ready to leave.

"Come on, Dad," the other child complained, "you talk too much."

My son nodded sympathetically. "Is your dad a preacher, too?"

Funny, he is.

∿

May 12 is the birthday of Edward Lear, a writer who popularized the limerick in 1846 with his *Book of Nonsense*. Every year in May, in the church where I serve as pastor, I write several limericks. I read a limerick for each of our elders and deacons who have completed their three-year term of service. I think Lear would delight at some of my nonsense—rhyming Sara with aloe vera, Donna with sauna, and Melissa with charisma. My favorite was the year I rhymed both John and Stan with pecan.

I started this practice at the first church I served. Everyone in that congregation called her Ms. Ann, but when she was the head nurse of the emergency room, she was known as Bulldog. Even in retirement, she remained tenacious and did not tolerate fools, including those who had recently graduated from seminary. On Monday morning, she would announce her presence with a strong knock on my pastor's study.

She served as an elder for three years. During her final meeting, I wrote and recited these words: *There once was an elder named Ms. Ann. She helped her young preacher understand, Though the Bible is a good story, not everything in the world is hunky-dory. Sometimes we need to take a stand.*

What utter nonsense! I still have the original copy, but only because Ms. Ann refused to take it with her. At least she laughed.

In the subsequent years, Ms. Ann suffered a series of ministrokes. Weak on her left side, she began to use a cane. With the tenacity of a bulldog, she insisted on coming to church on Sundays. However, she no longer visited my office during the week. Her son had taken her keys, which I imagine was a Herculean feat. Ms. Ann began to invite me to her home to drink strong coffee. I met her yappy little dog. When I left to serve another church, she gave me a firm handshake and then wiped a tear from her eye. I was crying freely.

As a pastor, I have watched parishioners lose ground, both physically and mentally. They have witnessed how I have lost hair and added gray to my beard. They have also seen my mistakes and omissions—words I failed to speak, actions I failed to take because I was anxious or afraid of what others might think. Ms. Ann and the rest of that congregation bore witness as I found my voice. Even though it was nonsense, my limerick was true: Ms. Ann helped teach me how to take a stand. According to the scripture, "As iron sharpens iron, so one person sharpens a friend."

A little more than five years after I had left, Ms. Ann's daughter reached out to say that her mother was too weak to talk on the phone but had a message for me: "Tell Andrew that I am going to see the place beyond the stars."

~

I just discovered that National Chicken Dance Day was actually *May* 14, not March 14—more awkward laughs![1]

This morning, I had physical therapy for my lower back, a muscle I'd pulled while spreading mulch in the yard. I couldn't stoop to put on my shoes for days—yes, *days* afterward. I had to admit that the physical therapy was helping. However, Kristen, my previous physical therapist, was preoccupied with other patients that morning, leaving me with a young college graduate who repeatedly referred to me as "my man," using phrases such as "Come on, my man, you can do it!" and "That's it, my man, one more!" Really, I should have been grateful for any of his attention because he was zeroed in upon a young woman who, though she was also having back pain, apparently needed far more of his time, meaning the dude was whining to her about his fender bender on his drive into work and, oh, the young woman said, she was sorry, *so sorry* for him, which only encouraged him to tell the story of the time when his car was totaled in a parking lot and how long it took him to collect the insurance money. Once they finally released me with a "See you next time, my man," I drove off, only to find myself stuck behind a work truck as it crawled through the neighborhood, making me even more late for work. I was cursing my luck when a woman approached me on the sidewalk. I could read her sweatshirt because I was moving so slowly: Allergic to Mornings. But when she caught my eye, instead of scowling or mumbling, or at least staring forlornly, she actually smiled and waved. A vigorous wave! She sure didn't seem allergic to mornings. Perhaps the sweatshirt was a joke, and she actually enjoyed being out and about, waving to complete strangers on their way to work; or perhaps she was generally in a bad mood but was having a particularly good day, such as when a friend called just to check

1. Of course, by the time you are reading this, I have revised this manuscript multiple times. I certainly could have changed the March entry. But here's the truth: I liked how that chapter turned out with it, which is to say, we make meaning out of our days, whether they are "official" national days or not.

in. Such a simple gesture can put a bounce in your step. Could the gleaming sun, beckoning high in the blue sky, be the source of her bright smile? Could it be the bluebirds singing on the wire?

This all occurred on May 14, which happens to be National No-Complaining Day.

Man, it was a beautiful day.

~

For Mother's Day, I gave Ginny a sleeveless T-shirt that read: Mama, Mommy, Mom, Bruh.

Bruh-itis has fully infected our eleven- and eight-year-old boys. Some days, it's every other word out of their mouths. Even the dog is learning to answer this name. Her name is Ramona, but she sits at Bruh, hoping the boy will reward her with a dog biscuit.

I'm learning how relationships evolve in more ways than just what we call each other. With our kids in school, she and I now work at the same church. The parishioners call her Rev. Ginny, and now our offices are side by side.

In addition to dividing responsibilities at church, we share more unpaid housework duties. One of my Mother's Day gifts was to clean out our minivan. Truth be told, this should happen more frequently. I have plenty of excuses; Ginny is exhausted of all of them.

I began by removing all the items that had accumulated on the van's floor. I was delighted to find not one, but two umbrellas, which I had presumed were missing. (So many of my former umbrellas are free agents.) Another notable find was the long-overdue library book. The vast majority of the floor's contents were shoved into an extra-duty trash bag. You don't need to be a forensic scientist to infer that my children primarily consume cereal bars and lollipops.

Now, the fun part—vacuuming! How satisfying to watch the cracker crumbs and dust bunnies disappear up the tube. Emptying the vacuum, I saw that I had collected enough dog hair to knit a lovely sweater. But I had other things to do, like rid the floor mats of unidentifiable sticky stuff.

Even though this was part of her present, Ginny pitched in to help, wiping the windows and dashboards. While the finished product was not up to the standards of a professional car detailer, she smiled with satisfaction.

The next day after church, we drove to my parents' neighborhood pool in Raleigh, and Ginny did a front flip off the diving board. She'd learned it back in high school. The boys and I were speechless. Their mama, mommy, mom, came out of the water, grinning like a little girl.

Bruh!

~

Like me, my wife, Ginny, has a younger brother, and we each spent our childhoods bossing them around. But we have each remained close to our brothers over the years. After we started dating, it became clear that we wanted our relationship to last, and we also knew that we wanted their support. Thankfully, Drew and John were gracious from the start, and the four of us remain friends to this day.

May 24 was declared National Brother's Day in 2005, which was the same year I first met Ginny. May 24 is also her birthday. Now that I know this connection, I celebrate two of the people I love most on the same day.

Growing up, John and I shared a love of sports. We played basketball on the hoop in our driveway and football with kids in the neighborhood. He and I spent countless hours throwing, catching, and hitting baseballs outside church, where our father was the pastor. One time, we managed to hit a baseball through the window of the pastor's office.[2]

At my wedding rehearsal dinner, John gave a homerun of a toast. My brother said that he had been thinking about a metaphor

---

2. Mea culpa. It was also my decision not to tell our father, which meant he discovered the broken window on Sunday morning. Mea maxima culpa.

as a blessing for our marriage, and he offered the image of hitting a baseball on the sweet spot of the bat. When you connect with a pitch just right, it's bliss.

June: Gratefully Tired

JUNE IS NATIONAL RIVERS Month. The Haw River runs a couple of miles south of my neighborhood. It's shallow near the bank. Once school is out for the summer, kids of all ages, including the young at heart, hop from rock to rock, making their way up or down the current. The object is to stay out of the water, except, of course, when you want to jump in with a splash. Rock-hopping is not a race. You can follow in someone's footsteps or leap on your own. For safety reasons, we strongly encourage wearing footwear, but uniforms are not required. The breeze rustles the leaves, while sunlight streams through braches, illuminating the shimmering water. Fish flash out of the way. Birdsong volleys overhead like laughter. Occasionally, someone may shriek at the sight of a water snake. It's likely not venomous. Move along, folks.

Occasionally, a rockhopper misjudges a leap and falls. Everyone rushes over to help. Usually, the person is fine; the cure involves more hopping.

~

The first Friday in June is National Donut Day, and I took my children to celebrate. There was a popular place about twenty miles away, so we loaded into the minivan only to have the kids fight the entire drive there. I gritted my teeth. I was trying to do something nice for them. And this is the "thanks" I get?

I was telling this story to Sarah Wiles, who's a mom, pastor, and fellow student in my doctoral program. Sarah admitted that she had had the same experience—not with donuts, but with trying to help her kids and failing. She told me about their Saturday morning ritual of making pancakes with various ingredients and toppings, which is really about sugar consumption. Quoting Sarah, "I hope I'm not setting them up for diabetes!" We laughed in the way that parents do—tired and grateful.

Sarah also wondered about what, if anything, her kids would remember. The "Mommy Morning Music" playlist? The impromptu dance parties? Will they remember the times when she was grouchy? Or when she chastised them for spilling flour and breaking eggs on the floor?

Oh, let my children remember not so much the hundreds, if not thousands, of times I said "no" with a short fuse and angry snarl, but the millions of ways beyond words that I lived "yes" in pickups and drop-offs, in snacks and treats, in smiles and bated breaths.

On National Donut Day, my kids and I finally arrived at the store and spilled out of the car. Racing ahead for the sugar consumption, their arguments were forgotten. I purchased the special, a baker's dozen. Let them pick their toppings. They each ate two donuts. I had one dusted with cinnamon and sugar. It was warm and sweet; my coffee was hot and strong. The children giggled as they watched the daytime commercials on the TV in the upper corner of the room. Oh, what will they remember?

～

On the last day of school, I sat in the carpool line, not paying much attention to an unfamiliar jazz tune on my radio. My mind returned to the office and my unfinished work. A boy strolled out of the school and yanked a yo-yo out of his pocket. Someone else besides me knew that June 6 is National Yo-Yo Day.

Or maybe this kid had a yo-yo every day. He was good. He spun the toy up and down a few times, then made a triangle out of the string with the yo-yo swinging back and forth. Another flick of his wrist, and the yo-yo spun at the end of the string, mere inches above the sidewalk. What a pro! The child's friends called to him, so he yanked it up and took off running.

June 6 was the birthday of Donald Franklin Duncan, founder of the Duncan Toys Company. The product tagline was "If it isn't a Duncan, it isn't a Yo-Yo." However, Duncan was not the toy's inventor. There are ancient Greek vase paintings from the mid-fifth century BCE that depict children playing with a version of the yo-yo. Versions of the toy date back to as early as 1,000 BCE in China.

"Yo-yo" is a cognate of a word in Tagalog, a language from the Philippines. It means "come and go" or "come back." In 1928, Pedro Flores, a Filipino immigrant, started the Yo-Yo Manufacturing Company in Santa Barbara, California. He made the first models by hand and personally taught the Filipino kids how to use them. Just a few years later, Duncan bought the company, including the naming rights, for $750,000—an astronomical sum in the Great Depression. Sixty years later, astronauts took the best-selling Duncan Imperials into space.

Since it was the last day of school, my kids would be over the moon. Far away, bombs were killing children. Just down the street from the school, a parishioner and friend was dying in hospice. Someone impersonating me had hacked the church's website earlier that week, defrauding people out of thousands of dollars. We are witnessing the melting of polar ice caps, the disappearance of forests in flames, and the sudden and permanent stillness of animal species.

The Latin word for "attention" means "to stretch toward," and I want to remain cognizant of the brutal while still aiming for the beautiful. Like that sparkling red yo-yo.

~

Juneteenth commemorates June 19, 1865, when the Union Army declared freedom for Black people enslaved in Texas. Over the past few years, I have participated in celebrations at the Black-owned fairgrounds on the outskirts of my community. Black artists and businesspeople set up stages and tents to showcase their talent and treasures. The food is amazing, the art incredible, and the music will get you moving.

During a performance by a step team from a local historically Black college, I saw Charles quietly grooving off to the side. My friend is one of the lead organizers of this Juneteenth celebration, yet he is a quiet man, preferring to work behind the scenes. Once he trusts you, he'll share stories from Jim Crow. A group of white students drowned a childhood friend. They claimed that they were only holding the child's head under the river as a joke. The police filed no charges.

How do you endure such pain without accountability or justice?

On Juneteenth, I saw Charles dance. When he caught me watching him, a wide smile shone from his face, and he threw up his hands as if to say, "Join me!" I tried my best.

∼

Hugh is a retired clergyman who came to church on Father's Day to ask me to read an essay he hoped to publish about his mid-career transition from a big steeple associate to the solo pastor of a rural congregation. Decades ago, he'd moved his wife and their young children into a manse adjacent to their little white clapboard church.[1]

After getting my kids to bed that night, I sat down with Hugh's essay: "Winds sang in the night, vibrating casement window strings up and down in glissando song." I had to look up

1. You know I love etymology, and "manse" shares the same root as "mansion," which makes most clergy shake their heads in disbelief. My first church, however, housed Ginny and me in a two-story farmhouse with plenty of room to grow our family. I don't expect to become rich as a pastor, but I remain grateful to both congregations I've served for their generosity and support.

glissando to learn it meant "a continuous slide upward or downward between notes." It involves blending rather than individually plucking or playing each note. In addition to his career in ministry, Hugh is an accomplished cello player.

I am not a trained musician, but I know the sound of night winds lying awake beside young children. A few days earlier, my younger son had asked in his darkened bedroom, "What does the wind say?" Before I could answer, he pursued his lips like he was trying to whistle and breathed loudly. When he inhaled, the sound slid higher; when he exhaled, it became lower and deeper.

"Dad, those are wind words."

Pay attention, I thought. *Remember this.* He and I breathed the wind's glissando song until both of us dropped off to sleep.

∿

Anticipating next month, World Jump Day is July 20. But on most rainy Saturday mornings after school is out for the summer, you will find dads of all shapes and sizes who have hauled their children to the indoor trampoline park. There are a few Bro Dads—dudes who wear sleeveless workout shirts to show off their biceps.

Other guys are Rover Dads. Their job is to fetch. But instead of sticks or balls, Rover Dad doggedly pursues his little kids over and around all the trampolines, picking them up after each face plant and snagging them moments before they launch themselves off a high jump. Rover Dad puts his own body at risk to protect his toddler from the tweens while they are taking selfies. Just ten minutes into the morning, Rover Dad is already exhausted. He's worked up more of a sweat than Bro Dad. That afternoon, his kid is going to have to put him down for a nap. I have been there.

But on this rainy Saturday, I do not need to chase toddlers. I am not jumping on trampolines. I have on my Birkenstocks (a Father's Day present to myself). I sneaked Starbucks into the forbidden bounce area and discreetly settled into a chair in a corner, where I could watch my kids and simultaneously check my phone for last night's NBA highlights (sad that Lebron couldn't win one more). Then I watch my kids with amusement as they play dodgeball on the trampolines—my youngest can hold her own with her brothers. I close my eyes and rest. My coffee is good, and so is life.

July: Sticky Grace

INTERNATIONAL JOKE DAY IS July 1, the midpoint of the year, and one day before I Forgot Day. However, I Forgot Day does not refer to all the punchlines I can never remember. Sometime in the late 1990s or early 2000s (she can't recall the exact date), Gaye Anderson was a student advisor at Davenport University. The end of the college's spring semester was full of stress for her. She invented July 2 as a makeup day, a chance to apologize for all the holidays and anniversaries she'd forgotten. Anderson must have been fairly desperate; that spring, she had forgotten to celebrate her adult daughter's birthday as well as her own wedding anniversary.

I Forgot Day reminds me of one of my favorite childhood concepts: the do-over. Whether shooting basketball hoops or swinging a baseball bat, sometimes you need a second chance. We adults might not extend as many do-overs to each other.

There's a saying that, surely, but by the grace of God, go I, meaning that, if not for divine providence or maybe just dumb luck, I would have made the same mistake and forgotten my daughter's birthday and my wedding anniversary.

But it would be better for me to say, but by Ginny's grace! She is the planner and organizer, the purchaser of presents, the booker of venues, and the maker of reservations. If it were solely up to me, I might not forget our children's birthdays, but I would likely throw the celebrations together at the last minute. We could never eat at a decent restaurant without a 45-minute wait.

Theological grace does not negate our actions. That would be absurd. We cause harm to others through our actions and inaction. While we often associate sin with doing the wrong thing, we also often overlook doing the right thing. When Ginny calls me out, I can become defensive. I might point to another thing that I did (pick the kids up from school) instead of acknowledging what I failed to do (left the dirty dishes in the sink overnight so that there was a mess in the morning when she went to pack the lunches for school).

In terms of my marriage vows, I Forgot Day has caused me to reflect on grace. Ginny and I promised to love each other that day, knowing we would make mistakes. But our love is not conditional. If this is true of us, then, as the rabbis suggest, it must be even more true of God. Surely, such is grace.

～

My previous dog, Nikki Giovanni, hated July Fourth. She was not vehemently anti-patriotic. In fact, she liked to chase a baseball and eat apple pie!

She was terrified of fireworks.

At the time, we lived less than a mile from the fairgrounds. When the fireworks began, this poor pup would hide under the bed, her body shaking harder than the dishes in the cabinets with each loud blast.

Long before the country's founding, fireworks were in existence. As early as 200 B.C.E., the Chinese were heating bamboo stalks over coals until they burst with a bang. They thought the loud noise scared off evil spirits. Almost a thousand years later, Chinese alchemists accidentally created potassium nitrate—gunpowder—while searching for an elixir for immortality. Now that is a tragic irony.

Nikki has been dead for several years, and I hope that she rests in peace. I also hope that those of us still alive will strive to create a world where people only use gunpowder for celebrations and the only casualties are frightened house pets.

~

We will celebrate National Fried Chicken Day on July 6, following the Fourth of July. My maternal grandmother would fry chicken whenever we visited because her daughter was a vegetarian, and Gran was concerned that my younger brother and I weren't getting enough meat. Gran also served us hamburgers for breakfast.

In the South, a "vegetable" plate may include mashed potatoes with bacon bits on top. Like many aspects of Southern culture, fried chicken is an example of cross-cultural influence. Scottish immigrants brought the concept of frying chicken in oil with them, yet it was the slaves from West Africa who seasoned the batter, effectively creating the recipe that millions enjoy today.

But this was also characteristic of the South: white people claimed the tradition as their own and then depicted Black Americans as greedy beneficiaries. Coon Chicken Inn, a popular restaurant chain, featured a caricature of a Black man smacking his lips with foolish delight up until the mid-1950s. Dave Chappelle, the controversial comedic genius, has a joke about white people watching him eat fried chicken: "Look at him," Chapelle mimicked, "he loves it just like it said in the encyclopedia." Like all genius comedians, his point is serious.

My own kids are growing up in the South. My wife and I do not raise them to be vegetarians. If given the option, they would probably eat hamburgers for breakfast. They also enjoy fried chicken, especially our middle son; when he was younger, he called it "chicken with the skin on."

All three kids attend a public school in our neighborhood. While there are levels of economic and gender diversity among the student body, there are few children of color. I fear that, with the rise of racist tropes once again in America, my kids will ingest attitudes that are even more harmful than fried batter.

Thank God for the Plant. This is a collaborative space of local businesses, many of which are owned by people of color, located ten miles from our neighborhood. Crafters sell jewelry and wooden sculptures, and beekeepers offer honey and beeswax candles. A greenhouse offers native flora for purchase. There's a microbrewery that also bakes cookies. Additionally, a farm-to-table vegetarian restaurant and a food truck operate nearby, serving meat from pastured cows, pigs, and chickens.

On any given Friday summer evening at the Plant, kids of various ages and skin hues snatch bites of food from the picnic tables before running back into the grassy field to throw frisbees or roll down the hill. "Tag, you're it!" shouted a Black boy with two dimples, just like my blue-eyed, blond-haired daughter, who took a bite of her fried chicken before chasing her tagger with glee.

~

I'm thinking about stereotypes this month. The second Friday in July is National Motorcycle Day. My next-door neighbor has a gray-streaked mohawk and rides a huge, shiny green motorcycle. When I first got to know Forrest, he cut meat at a local grocery store during the nighttime "graveyard" shift and posted to social media amusing pictures of himself wielding a giant cleaver. At least, I thought they were hilarious; I trust Forrest. He can fix just about anything, including the backyard fence we share. He also takes care of Ramona, our house coyote, when my family goes out of town. He wooed her by slipping hot dogs over the fence.

My neighbor also went back to college and earned a professional license to repair motorcycles, transforming his hobby into gainful employment.

And Forrest, the very same mohawk-wearing, motorcycle-driving neighbor, is on a first-name basis with the first Black woman poet laureate of North Carolina. We had Jaki Shelton Green give a reading at church, and she welcomed Forrest into her arms with the biggest smile. It turns out that they used to be neighbors.

My neighbor rides his motorcycle to a biker bar off the highway, which in the past I have described as "sketchy." He describes the gathering of tattooed, shaved-headed, leather-wearing bikers as "sweet guys."

Humans are tribal and tend to stick to our own. I like to attend poetry readings. I drive a Prius. But I love my nextdoor neighbor, and because of him, I don't look at bikers the same way.

Last summer, I was in Pittsburgh studying theology when a burly dude pulled his road hog outside the seminary. Years ago, I would have walked a little faster. This time, I asked this biker if he needed help. He was looking for directions, which I was able to give using the GPS on my phone. We shook hands. As he pulled away with the roar of his engine, I smiled to myself. What a sweet guy.

⁓

In 1975, there were a grand total of 40 registered tattoo parlors. In just five years, that number had exploded to 5,000. In 2023, there were over 26,000 businesses and roughly 45 million Americans with tattoos. National Tattoo Day is the unofficial celebration of all things inked on the body.

The practice of body art is actually ancient. The Swiss Alps preserved a five thousand-year-old human with 61 tattoos on his body. The process of creating these tattoos involved cutting the skin and then inserting charcoal beneath the flesh. The Old Testament law in Leviticus 19:28 prohibited this form of tattoo: "You shall not make gashes in your flesh or incise any marks on yourselves." The Levitical, or "Purity Code," primarily aimed to differentiate the religious practices of the ancient Israelites from those of neighboring cultures.

However, Revelation 19:16 describes the Risen Lord Jesus as riding a white horse and having the phrase "King of kings and Lord of lords" tattooed on his thigh.

Many Christians, including pastors and laypeople, ink Bible verses, sometimes in Greek or Hebrew, the original written languages of the ancient scriptures. People also depict other religious symbols. My father's church once employed a secretary with a neck tattoo of a Chinese letter. She joked that it meant, "You will regret this."

I have no plans for a tattoo, and I don't think I'll ever regret this choice. Yet, their popularity has helped me better appreciate the art and even see its beauty. To quote the famous Russian novelist, Dostoevsky, "Beauty will save the world." That would not be a bad tattoo, whether on your body or simply in your memory.

~

Half of a dead pig, usually cut into slabs of bacon, is known as a "flitch." This has to do with celebrating faithfulness in marriage, obviously!

In medieval England, sometime in the twelfth or fifteenth centuries (sources vary), wealthy nobles began to hang a flitch in the entrance hallway of their manor. (This gives me a new appreciation for mistletoe.) A couple from the surrounding area could come and ask for the flitch on the day after their one-year wedding anniversary if they promised that they had never regretted their union—not even once in the past 365 days. They summoned a jury, usually composed of monks, to ascertain their truthfulness. The couple was often required to swear oaths while kneeling on sharp stones in the church graveyard. The flitch served as a reward for their trustworthiness.

In this country, Flitch Day, on July 19, commemorates the ritual by telling wacky history. Perhaps it's just an excuse to eat bacon.

In the first year of our marriage, Ginny and I were both vegetarians. We ate soy-based products that resembled meat in the way that the Olive Garden serves Italian food; in both instances, you would be better off filling up on bread sticks. After trying plant-based bacon, I took to eating plain tomato sandwiches instead of faux-BLTs.

She and I now eat meat, including bacon, on the rare occasion when we can pry a strip or two from our carnivorous children, who could consume an entire flitch and probably ask for more.

There is a line attributed to various people about never considering divorce but instead contemplating the murder of one's spouse. Very medieval. I appreciate the quote from Anne Lamott: "A good marriage is where both people feel like they're getting the better end of the deal."

A couple of years ago, I promised to give Ginny a card every Wednesday of the upcoming year. I might have missed a week or two (don't make me swear oaths while kneeling on sharp stones). But it was fun and often made her smile. She has kept a few of these cards, mostly the silly ones, and even now I'll discover she is using one to mark her place in her book.

Last year, my beloved gave me a card with a picture of a piece of smiling bacon. Upon opening the card, music began to play, and a strip of bacon, donning sunglasses, crooned, "I love you more than bacon, and I really love bacon!" We kept this card in a place of honor on the windowsill so that the kids could play it after supper for months on end. They played it until the battery died.

To celebrate Flitch Day, I went looking for a bacon card. I came across numerous puns, such as "Don't go bacon my heart; you are bacon me crazy," but none were as amusing as the musical card that Ginny gifted me years ago. In this and so many other ways, I am the one getting the better end of this deal.

～

My only brother lives in New Jersey. Due to the distance and time constraints, I manage to see John just a couple of times a year. It's challenging to account for our schedules, including the needs of work and our young children. My three kids have only met their nephew a couple of times at my parents' home in Raleigh.

This July, we planned a trip to our ancestors' family farm in eastern Pennsylvania. My day's cousin had restored and updated the farmhouse with electricity and indoor plumbing. We drove up from North Carolina, and my brother came down with his son. It was Monday, July 24, which just so happens to be National Cousins Day—I can't make this stuff up.[1]

The Latin word for cousin means "mother's sister's child." In English, the term came to include your uncle's kids as well as your siblings'. The prefix co- means "to join together," such as in words like coalition, coalesce, coincide, and coordinate. A few generations ago, it was easier for cousins to get together because families lived in close proximity.

Granted, the passage of time has brought advantages (indoor plumbing). However, the increasing mobility of Americans has led to a loss of the sense of connection that accompanies a strong sense of place. Families, like mine, struggle to gather across distances.

Don't worry if July 24 passed without your knowledge. Schedule a time with your cousin that works for you. Your plans don't have to be grand. There is magic in simplicity.

On the land where my family has gathered since the early nineteenth century, the young cousins spent the afternoon of July 24 in the creek that runs through the property. At three-and-a-half years old, my nephew is a self-styled crawdad hunter. My older children agreeably yielded to their little cousin's expertise and splashed through the shallow water, overturning rocks according to his instructions. They also built bridges and dams. On the bank, they climbed the larger rocks and found heart-shaped patches of moss. Though they caught only mosquito bites, they came running back to the house with wide grins.

That evening, I built a fire in the yard's outdoor stone circle. We roasted marshmallows. We made s'mores with Hershey's chocolate (we were in Pennsylvania). While I can't confirm my nephew's crawdad hunting skills (or this animal's residence in the mountains of eastern Pennsylvania), I witnessed his sticky fingers extended toward his relatives as he exclaimed, "All these people love me!"

---

1. There are many serendipities in this book. See the next chapter and August 18!

August: Happy Accidents

August 2 is Dinosaur Day. While they ruled the world hundreds of millions of years ago, these prehistoric creatures continue to rule the imagination of my children, who devour information about dinosaurs in books, movies, TV shows, and art projects, all of which leads me to the second celebration . . .

August 2 is National Coloring Book Day. My youngest loves to color everything, from these extinct reptiles[1] to Disney princesses to fearsome tigers.

If these scientific and artistic adventures leave you hungry, never fear. August 2 is also National Ice Cream Sandwich Day. Children of all ages know exactly how to celebrate.

~

August 3 is National Grab Some Nuts Day. No further comment.

It also happened to be the first Saturday that marked National Disc Golf Day. I knew two guys who played a weekly round of Frisbee. Though I hadn't played since my undergraduate days,

---

1. My sons informed me that the dinosaur was actually more closely related to birds. In the North Carolina Museum of Natural History, I learned that Tyrannosaurus rex is a closer cousin to chickens than alligators. Just outside our neighborhood, there is a chicken coop with a ferocious rooster named Prince, who has terrified my kids and me. The science makes sense to me.

this seemed like a wonderful opportunity to spend time with them. When I wondered if I could tag along, they graciously agreed.

The 18-hole course winding through the woods was a pleasure to walk. It was cooler in the shade, and the air was not as sticky. Most of my throws ended up among the trees and underbrush off the well-maintained path. But between our groans about wayward frisbees and the occasional hurrah of a well-thrown disc, we talked about stuff that matters: our families, childhoods, and church. After a few holes, I smiled and told them that I was enjoying this. I had just chucked yet another disc off a large oak, but they knew I wasn't talking about just the game itself.

I played a little disc golf back in college, but hanging out with friends was never a problem in those days. There were intramural sports, parties, and cafeterias. There were guys just lounging around in the dorm, playing Mario Kart. So-called "adulting," which includes marriage, parenthood, and career, has brought many beautiful and rewarding aspects to my life. It's also true that now I need to make much more of an effort to hang out with other guys my age.

I played nine holes that morning before I needed to get back home. I joked in the parking lot that I would love to participate in the game the following week, even if I had to throw left-handed due to my sore arm.

~

I got into a conversation with an older white man the other day in a church fellowship hall. We were there as part of a group working for racial justice and equity. He told me that he was recently on a plane home and struck up a conversation with the young Black man seated next to him. It turned out that they lived only a few miles apart. When the plane landed, the older guy invited him to his house to play pickleball.

Pickleball?

National Pickleball Day is August 8. I admit that I have made fun of this sport. The diminutive court, the dinky paddle, and, of course, the absurd moniker all contribute to this mockery. Not to mention the preponderance of gray-haired folks who sing the game's praises until they sprain an ankle or worse. Orthopedic surgeons have never had greater job security. Still, this guy solemnly swore, "Pickleball is a blessing." He seemed like a reasonable guy, not one to drink the Pickle-Aid.

But pickleball?!

The fact was that this seemingly silly sport brought two men together across generational and racial divisions, overcoming barriers that more venerable, perhaps socially esteemed activities (like church) had failed to do. The proof was in the (pickle) pudding.

I reached out to my fellow pastor at the historically Black church where our group met. He and I agreed to play at our new friend's house. It turned out that I have a lot to learn. I need to study up on the non-volley zone and learn what constitutes a foot fault. There are dinks and drops, punches, and slammers—all in fun, of course. There are kitchens, falafel, and flapjacks, but no eating on the court. Volley llamas are illegal. Too bad.

I realize that I have blind spots and assumptions based on my own experiences, which leaves me biased against more than just pickleball. I am committed to cross-cultural dialogue and intentional conversations about race.

However, I'm worn out by the constant hand-wringing from well-meaning individuals. I'm "tired," as in the Langston Hughes poem by that title, and like him, I'm ready to do something "good and beautiful and kind." I know there are problems in my community. I want to do something! Consider picking up a paddle instead of a racquet. Even though it sounds like Wiffle Balls are mating, I can testify that I had fun, didn't tear my ACL, and made new friends. Pickleball really is a blessing. Amen.

∽

For as long as I can remember, the birthday tradition in my family included serving a piece of cake on a shiny red plate emblazoned with the words YOU ARE SPECIAL. Mom made sure that both my younger brother and I received our own plates after John and I married our wives, so that we could carry on the tradition in our new homes.

Like me, Ginny has a younger brother. Like everyone else, we firstborns have baggage, but lack of attention is rarely one of them. We tend to think that the special plate was made for us.

National Middle Child Day is meant to shine a light on the child most often overlooked. There is a movement to change the celebration to July 2, which is the exact middle of the calendar year. Yet, many middle children worry that Independence Day on July 4 will overshadow their event. Wouldn't that be typical?

The day before National Middle Child Day happens to be my brother-in-law's birthday. Ginny and I drove to Virginia to celebrate Drew at a minor league baseball game. He had rented one of the suites above the grandstand for twenty of his friends. Milling around and making small talk, I asked folks where they were from and what they did. I also inquired about their siblings. When I met a guy who was a middle child, I eagerly told him about the national day. (It turns out that I have become that guy.) He just shrugged: "If there's a holiday that no one celebrates, is it really a holiday?"

Even if it's doubtful that National Middle Child Day will rise to the level of a birthday, I made sure we left Drew's house the next morning with enough time to go to the local co-op. I purchased a chocolate éclair. I got cupcakes for our other kids, but the éclair (with creamy pudding in the middle) was for the middle child. I placed the éclair on the YOU ARE SPECIAL plate, with a tall, sparkly candle in between two short blue candles. When my mom brought my kids back home, I was prepared.

Our middle child lit up when he saw the special celebration for him.

But Mom, innocent of my plans, had gotten them giant cookies on the ride to our house. Let the record show that her intentions were good. Mom is also a middle child. Besides, she is Nana.

But after the second round of treats, all three children ended up with stomach aches and barely touched their supper. Poking at his dinner, the eldest complained, "When is it my special day?" I pointed out that he had three whole years before his sibling's birth, during which we dedicated every single day to him. I meant it as a joke, but no one even smiled.

Then the oldest, without any prompting, declared that his brother got to pick the after-supper family game. Ever the peacemaker, the middle child picked dodgeball, which is actually his brother's favorite game. We play a game similar to freeze tag, and in this particular instance, the middle child took the lead. This meant that he was the center of attention. He feigned a throw in one direction, spun around, and hurled the ball straight off my forehead. I tried to stay frozen, but I was laughing too hard.

∿

"Serendipity" is a delicious word to say. Serendipity can feel like the stars have all aligned, or simply that something fell into place at the right time. My favorite definition is "happy accident." Serendipity is about timing.

Not knowing that August 18 was National Serendipity Day, Ginny bought tickets for our entire family to the performance of a live drama featuring giant handmade puppets created out of paper mâché, cardboard, cornstarch, and bamboo. I pulled our minivan to the curb so the rest of my family could hustle into the Forest Theatre, an outdoor venue on the campus of the University of North Carolina at Chapel Hill. Then I parked about a half-mile away. I was trying to figure out how to pay for parking when I heard my name. A fellow dad and his daughter walked up.

I knew him because his daughter was friends with mine at their preschool. As we made our way to the show, we exchanged pleasantries and talked about the weather. He asked if I happened to know any other Troutmans. I shrugged. It's a fairly common name. There's even a town called Troutman in North Carolina.

"When I was in school here, I knew a guy named John Troutman."

That was my younger brother's name. He also went to Carolina. This guy knew my brother and dated the same woman! Not at the same time, mind you, but my brother had a painful breakup, including the fact that this ex-girlfriend had quickly moved on to another dude—the guy standing right next to me.

It turned out that this guy was well aware of that connection, including the tension that it caused twenty years ago.

"Funny how things work out," he commented.

I grinned. "You know, in college, I didn't even know your name. But there was a time when I hated your guts." We chuckled.

Serendipity causes me to think of the theology of God's providence, which, in the hands of John Calvin and others, led to ideas like predestination, where God is a monster who condemns people to eternal punishment before they were even born, even from the foundation of time. That's crazy.

I don't believe that God controls our every movement like a puppeteer. The divine plan's genius is giving us autonomy so we can act from our personal goodness, the divine spark.

But "a happy accident" seems like a higher purpose's wink, if not a plan. It's fun, and maybe more theology should coax a smile. I'll say this—so much of life is about timing.

The show was fantastic. Our daughter spent most of the show seated with her friend from her preschool, while her dad and I relaxed together, taking in the beautiful sights and happy accidents.

~

A friend's Golden Retriever nipped our two-year-old middle child's nose shortly after we moved to Chapel Hill in 2018. This old dog was mild-mannered but didn't see very well. My son had unwittingly surprised her. There was just a little blood, but a lot of crying. Though his skin healed quickly, he spent years being afraid, and his siblings began to mimic him. If they saw a dog coming toward them on the sidewalk, they would cross to the other side of the street.

When we were thinking about adopting a pet, we thought more knowledge about dogs would help ease our children's anxiety. Ginny purchased a picture book, *First Friend*, that describes the evolution of the domestic canine from wolves. I learned that, over tens of thousands of years, our relationship to the wild species developed into cohabitation by hunting together and sharing food.

In the modern world, many people look to dogs for emotional support. They are our best friends, or "fur babies." We feed them, shelter them, and exercise them. Maybe we could dress them in adorable dog sweaters with gnome images and the slogan "Chilling with My Gnomes" (another of Ginny's purchases).

A woman named Colleen Paige created National Dog Appreciation Day in 2004 to encourage canine adoption. (In fairness to other animal lovers, she also founded National Pet Day on April 11.) Paige chose August 26 because on that day, when she was 10 years old, her family brought home a Sheltie. I appreciate the focus of this national day on rescue animals, for I imagine that many of these creatures have endured trauma.

In return, a dog can teach a child about unconditional love. Dogs continue to evolve with us as we learn, struggle, heal, and, hopefully, move toward wholeness. They love us when we change. Similar to the National Day of Tenderness in January, National Dog Appreciation Day has prompted me to consider the concept of reciprocity—our care for each other, particularly as we undergo various changes.

When my family selected our dog from a shelter, we named her Ramona in homage to our favorite literary heroine, Ramona Quimby—Beverly Cleary's scrappy, intelligent, sometimes rebellious girl. As a puppy, Ramona experienced abandonment in the woods. Who knows what she had to endure in order to survive?

The fictional Ramona Quimby spoke the truth: "It wasn't fair that life was not fair." At some point, we all experience trauma, bearing the consequences of our actions or the pain resulting from events beyond our control.

What we can do is look directly at our fear. It is a gift to have people and pets stand beside us, walk with us, and look at us with love. Tender the ways.

Though our rescue dog is two years old—that's fourteen in human years, as the kids always add—Ramona is still a puppy, which is my way of telling you that she tears around the house in what the kids have termed The Zoomies. She's wild. After a few months, I started referring to her as the house coyote. She chases all adorable things: squirrels, rabbits, and the seven-year-old boy down the street.

However, when one of us is sick, Ramona takes on a new role.

My daughter had a low-grade fever, and as she fell asleep on the couch, the house coyote became Nurse Doggie. All afternoon, Ramona lay next to her. Once, my daughter cried out in her sleep, and Ramona nosed her ever so gently. Just making sure of her. When my girl went back to sleep, Ramona sighed. I watched them both fall back asleep.

After her nap, my daughter was a new person. (Amazing how kids can bounce back.) She dumped the couch cushions to play Floor Is Lava. Then the boys came home from school, and Ramona joined the joyful melee.

September: & Joy

On September 2, 2007, a bright blue canvas of sky stretched over Richmond, Virginia. The sun beamed upon the sunflowers arranged in my bride's long, golden hair.

Over the years, we've celebrated our wedding anniversaries at bed and breakfasts or in a tiny home in the Blue Ridge Mountains, enjoying brief moments of luxury. When we set our sights closer to home and went out to dinner, I tried to spruce up the festivities with flowers and jewelry. I've written a few (sappy) poems.

This year, I celebrated our anniversary in true National Hummingbird Day style, with not only a hummingbird card but also sparkling earrings—ruby-throated hummingbirds, so named for the iridescent red throat. Ginny laughed: "I didn't know sixteen was the year of the hummingbird!"

According to WeddingWire.com, the traditional gift for the sixteenth year is wax. We agreed my selection was preferable.

∽

I have kept a beard for our entire marriage. There was one night in seminary when, along with some fellow classmates, I shaved for Sketchy Mustache Night. Ginny, who I was dating at the time, took one look at me and burst into tears. Although I have been threatening to shave again for Mo-vember (mustaches in November to raise awareness for men's health), I am teasing her. There is always National Beard Day on September 5.

The summer before I met Ginny, I was serving as a youth director and led a group of teenagers and adults to work in Harlan County, Kentucky. We helped put siding on a dilapidated trailer. There were big black balloons of trash bags scattered across the dirt yard. Ralph could barely hobble down the steps due to a back injury he had sustained in the coal mines. He had a long, red beard that flowed down his chest. After a week, I sported a decent stubble on my face. The last time I saw him, Ralph shook my hand. "Remember me, will you?" When we returned, I kept the beard as a tribute to him. Then I met Ginny. She liked the beard right away. Our kids have never seen anything different on their dad's face. Even with the addition of white hair, I still appreciate its appearance.

Since then, I've led other youth trips to the Appalachian Mountains, as well as large cities. Though poverty is different from place to place, the people are often nameless. Discussed as numbers. Highlighted as a problem. We obscure, dismiss, and denigrate the real people. In my university town, I could seal myself in my neighborhood and social circles without getting to know anyone who is actually struggling with food or housing security.

But in addition to the trips and volunteer opportunities in our community, I receive requests for help at church. Some days, the office phone rings right before I go home for dinner with my family. There is a moment when I am tempted to let the call go to voicemail. I might rub my beard, though, and remember how Ralph taught me to play Pink Floyd's "Wish You Were Here" on his old Fender guitar. Then I will answer the phone.

◦∾◦

The second Tuesday of September is National Ants on a Log Day, which we observe in our home by spreading peanut butter on bananas and adorning raisins on top. I realize that others use celery and craisins, even cream cheese. Heathens.

My daughter and I are the only members of our family who appreciate all three traditional ingredients, so she was an obvious choice to join me in celebrating. Now a kindergartener, she's gaining more and more independence, including in the kitchen. She insisted on spreading her own peanut butter, some of which actually got on the banana. It was an enormous mess, but I hugged her and expressed my admiration for her effort.

Two days later, National Ampersand Day occurred. Because "et" means "and" in Latin, I learned that the glyph is a ligature or combination of the letters e and t (e & t). William Blake popularized the ampersand in English. Not only was Blake a poet, he was also a painter and printmaker, and he would illustrate his verses with beautiful calligraphy. In Blake's hands, the ampersand was a work of art.

Unlike many of their peers, my kids learn to write in cursive as part of their Montessori[1] school curriculum. Recent studies have investigated the positive effects of cursive writing on fine motor skills, as well as stimulating the brain to make deeper connections with language. My children take far more pride in their handwriting skills than me. In fact, they tease me about my chicken scratch script.

Often, after an afternoon snack, my daughter will invite me to draw with her at the kitchen table. We pull out crayons and colored pencils. She places a blank sheet before me. She commands, "Now, draw!" I've taken to doodling ampersands, sometimes in a Blake line: "I am in you & you in me, mutual divine love."

My daughter inspected my work. She gave me a hug. "I'm proud of you for trying."

~

---

1. The Italian physician, educator, and namesake of the modern pedagogical movement was an amazing woman, and this is not lost on my children. After a few weeks of school, my son inquired why we didn't have a picture of Dr. Montessori hanging on the wall at church. Hail, Maria, full of grace!

Somehow, I missed the fact that September 12 is both National Video Game and National Chocolate Milkshake Day, but my children get screen time and sweets on a regular basis.

But the following day, I was thinking about National Positive Thinking Day because, over the past month, I've seen a dozen red-tailed hawks. Not only have I seen the soaring raptors while I've hiked, but I've also spotted these birds while driving on my typical errands. I'll happen to look up and spot a hawk scowling like a judge from a telephone pole, or catch a glimpse of one zipping through the air like a knife thrown into a tree. I began to wonder if these sightings were a message from God or some omen about the future. Native Americans on this land, like the Iroquoi and Sioux, believed hawks were messengers from other worlds and signs of good health. I asked Ginny what she thought my sightings might mean one night after we'd gotten the kids to bed and were relaxing on the couch.

She told me that I was seeing lots of hawks precisely because I was looking for hawks.

Christians and other believers, as part of the manifestation movement, believe you can imagine and create your future. A bit like Thoreau's "Go confidently in the direction of your dreams." I'm inclined to think of positive thinking in terms of Wendell Berry, one of my favorite writers: "Be joyful even though you have considered all the facts."[2] The facts are troubling, even terrifying, like the rise in global temperatures, sea levels, and school shootings. Just as field mice should be worried about hawks, humankind should likewise be concerned about climate change and gun violence. Berry's wisdom implies that joy is not separate from worry or even sorrow. Although we cannot control everything, we can choose what to focus on. We can decide to consider both the negative and the positive. The glass encompasses not just its liquid contents but also its entirety.

This time of year marks the autumnal equinox, meaning the end of summer and the beginning of fall. Leaves turn colors,

2. From Berry's famous poem, "Manifesto: The Mad Farmer Liberation Front"

sunlight grows dimmer, and mornings feel crisper. Currently, my beard is changing colors and my top hair is falling out. Yet, there are also signs of new beginnings. Not only is there yellow on the treetops, but also on the bright buses. Children skip and twirl down the sidewalks, like fallen leaves in the wind. What will I focus on? Have you ever seen a hawk drop like a knife from the sky? It takes my breath away.

~

I went to check out my groceries at the co-op. The clerk wore a tri-corner hat with the image of the Jolly Roger, the infamous skull and crossbones. One never knows what to expect at the quirky, friendly neighborhood co-op. He opened his mouth and talked like a pirate, rolling his Rs and calling me a "scallywag" as he loaded my reusable shopping bags. It was delightful! National Talk Like a Pirate Day is September 19.

On the University of North Carolina campus, county and state officials spoke like pirates as they passed out information to students about emergency preparation, such as CPR classes and fire extinguisher manuals. This puts a silly national day to good use; it's a schtick for a higher cause.

But I don't need such lofty purposes. As they boarded the minivan after school, I greeted my children with, "Arrrrrrrren't you glad school is over?"

My older son was not amused. "Dad, is this another one of your weird day of the year things again?"

"You arrrrrrrrrrrrrre correct, Matey!"

~

September 21 is International Peace Day, a 24-hour ceasefire first declared by the United Nations General Assembly in 2001. At a PTA event for my children's elementary school, they asked me to mark the occasion with a few words. One doesn't wish to belabor the point; the kids are waiting on the pizza. But I had to inform the gathering that September 21 was also Miniature Golf Day (though not by decree of the United Nations).

My kids and I take turns whacking a multicolored ball across fake grass at a course at the beach. Last summer, both my sons hit a hole-in-one. And my five-year-old daughter won an air guitar contest! When the deejay invited participants in the contest, she jumped at the chance—she jumped up and down, waving her toy inflatable guitar in the air, racing around the putting green to Guns 'N Roses, Metallica, and ACDC.

Peacemaking is also an active effort. Unlike sinking a hole-in-one or winning a contest, we may not receive immediate rewards. However, we use our various gifts for the common good. Some love the spotlight, while others prefer to be behind the scenes. We have diverse cultures, religions, and philosophies. We can all work for peace. As Archbishop Desmond Tutu said, "Do your little bit of good where you are; it's those little bits of good together that overwhelm the world." As I told the PTA gathering, rock on!

~

When I learned that September 24 was National Bluebird of Happiness Day, I immediately thought of a certain bluebird who flies from the trees behind my home each morning for the sole purpose of leaving his calling cards dripping down on my Prius. It seems to make him happy that he splattered the car door handle on the driver's side.

I learned that the Chinese word for bluebird is a homophone for the Chinese word for "happiness." According to Benedictine monk David Steindl-Rast, "Happiness does not lead to gratitude. Gratitude leads to happiness."

My seminary classmate, Scarlett, often quoted Steindl-Rast on her Facebook page. While she was battling ovarian cancer, she would post his pithy sayings about gratitude and other spiritual virtues. Before she got sick, she sat next to me in Hebrew class. I complained about the verb tenses. I thought that we had all the time in the world; in fact, I wished time would move faster so that I could get out of class.

Scarlett's Facebook page outlived her. I can still pull up images of her watercolors (she was a fantastic painter) and inspirational quotes from mystic leaders of Buddhism and Christianity, including Steindl-Rast. She was dying, and she knew it. She still posted pictures of gorgeous flower arrangements gifted by members of her congregation, as well as small birds stopping by her patio.

This morning, in addition to the bluebird's calling cards, I witnessed a honey glow in the air from the rising sun. There was a brisk chill more invigorating than my cup of coffee. I paused before opening my car door and gave thanks. I felt this happiness and joy.

~

Bluebirds have inspired me to think more about hummingbirds.

Brian Doyle's essay about hummingbirds, "Joyas Voladoras," is about their amazing beauty. It is also about death: "Consider for a moment those hummingbirds who did not open their eyes again today... each thunderous wild heart the size of an infant's fingernail, each mad heart silent, a brilliant music stilled."[3]

Three years ago, a friend of mine died unexpectedly. Following Ron's graveside service, I slumped against the back of the columbarium wall. He'd been among the happiest people I knew—his retirement was filled with golf, UNC men's basketball games, and five glorious grandchildren. Plus, he had rocked out at over fifty Rolling Stones concerts. Now, his life was "brilliant music stilled." My head was in my hands, but I happened to glance up.

A shimmer in the trees. A dart here, a flash there. The hummingbird zigzagged toward me until it hovered less than six feet over my head. He was close enough for me to see his blurred wings and iridescent red throat. The bird looked down, cocked his head, and winked.

Winked?!

3. Doyle, 3–4

Later, I learned that hummingbirds were manifestations of gods for the Aztecs and Hopi. The Cherokee believed they were messengers from loved ones beyond the grave.

That day, as the hummingbird zoomed over my head, I scrambled to my feet, twisting to follow his flight and already wondering—in both senses of that word—if that wink had actually happened.

~

I favor smaller apples because I eat the core and all. Although committed to the task, I'll readily admit that there is usually a bite that you have to chew without pleasure, generally due to the starchiness of the core. It helps if you don't bite down on the seeds, which will tinge even the sweetest ambrosia apple with bitterness.

I use the same skills I've honed in countless baseball dugouts to separate the seeds from the apple in my mouth. Now, I spit the apple seed in the grass. Who knows? Maybe a few will take root. Like a modern Johnny Appleseed, will my scatterings from the window of my minivan grow into trees along a highway?

At the neighborhood trailhead, I recently deposited a seed. My daughter carefully buried it. When finished, she gave the tiny mound of dirt a blessing—pat, pat—before running into the woods, yelling for me to catch her. She jumped into a puddle and sprayed my pants all the way up my leg just as I caught up. I faked anger: "Oh, you better run now!" We took off in the trail's dappled light, laughing. It was September 26, National Johnny Appleseed Day, and Oh, the Lord's been good to me.

October: Suffer Gladly

In this country, there are only two types of people: those who love pumpkin-flavored foods and those married to people who love pumpkin-flavored foods. Dutifully, I told my wife that October was Pumpkin Spice Month. Of course, these flavored items have been available since Labor Day.

As I helped Ginny unload groceries from her most recent trip, I lined up the following on the counter: pumpkin Cheerios, pumpkin cereal bars, pumpkin spaghetti sauce, pumpkin soup, pumpkin salsa, and cans of pumpkin for pumpkin pancakes.

My lovely bride sighed. "I really showed some restraint."

Our little pumpkin heads have inherited their mother's tastes. Like a lot of dads, I am a scavenger at the kitchen table, feeding on our brood's leftovers. In the morning, I slurp their soggy cereal, and later in the day, I scrape their vegetables onto my dinner plate.

When we serve pumpkin flavors, my kids drink their bowls dry and lick their plates clean.

Only the house coyote sides with me. In order to help with digestion, our vet recommended a scoop of pumpkin in her dry dog food. But though Ramona is colorblind, our dog refuses to eat the orange.

After unloading the groceries, I leashed the pumpkin hater, and we walked underneath the fall colors, enjoying the chill in the air and dreaming of all things bacon.

∽

I love garlic; it doesn't love me. Or, more honestly, my beloved people don't love that I eat garlic. Ginny will tell you—the smell comes out of my pores. Not only do I have garlic breath, but I also suffer from garlic *stank*. She and I have been together for over 18 years. I tell her, "You are long suffering." She smiles. Sometimes.

How does she suffer? Let me count the ways: garlic stank, obviously; my habit of singing children's songs at random times (Casper Babypants, "Stompy the Bear"); my tendency to leave dirty dishes in the sink overnight; how I inform her about an evening meeting as we sit down for supper; and let's not forget how I clog the shower drain with my hair. For years, she dreamed of double sinks in our bathroom. But now that this blessing has come to pass, she still discovers my shavings in her sink. Those little hairs appear to be intrepid explorers, spanning entire continents of porcelain.[1]

We've also upgraded to a king-sized bed with sheets so large that I can't even steal all of them with one midnight swoop in my sleep. This October, as per usual, we took the kids camping and spent the night on a twin-size air mattress. The next morning, I wanted to mimic a ritual from Robin Wall Kimmerer's *Braiding Sweetgrass* and pour out the first of the coffee as a thank-you offering. Ginny growled, "Give it to me!"

This year, I marked National Garlic Lovers Day (October 6) by reading the garlic essay in Ross Gay's *Book of (More) Delights*. He's delighted by the first green shoots from the soil in spring. Gay wrote that he has had success growing garlic for a dozen straight years; he's batting a thousand. Then he corrected himself—the garlic is doing all the work. He just handed over the bat.

I hope that Ginny won't hit me with any blunt objects.

Marriage is a partnership (duh), and not all things are equal. You compromise, you sacrifice, and you have fun. If I can hit some pitches alone, the family team benefits. Though National

---

1. Robert Hass has a poem, "Habits of Paradise," that begins, "Maybe if I made the bed, / it would help," which I have adopted as my New Year's resolution.

Pizza Day is actually February 9, I make pizza every Friday. I shop for all the ingredients, make the dough, cook the pies, serve the slices, and clean up. It's Ginny's night to relax and watch a movie with the kids.

Yes, I often sauté garlic with the mushrooms.

∽

Many of these national days I've either observed by myself or *inflicted* upon my immediate family.[2] The entire neighborhood celebrated National Walk to School Day on the first Wednesday in October. Even before I thought to alert the PTA, they had already planned it.

After getting coffee with my friend Brent, he asked, "What's up with all these 'national days'?" He made exaggerated air quotes, like little bunnies hopping along. "Why do you require such a day? Can't you walk to school anytime?"

Feeling somewhat defensive, I replied that the idea of a national day, even if it is silly, is to highlight something. It stands to reason that a National Walk to School Day will result in more ambulation among parents and students.

Granted, walking to school means getting my kids out the door 15 minutes earlier than usual. But I have to tell you, Brent, it's worth it.

We met up with a gaggle of parents and students at the local park, about a mile from the school's campus. The place was a hive of excitement. Kids were high-fiving, hugging, and squealing with laughter. Taking selfies, two-sies, and three-sies. There were PTA presidents organizing group photos for social media (#WalkToSchoolDay). The sheriff's department assigned a half dozen officers to direct traffic.

My kindergartener had already declared, "I'm just in it for the dogs." She was not disappointed. My little girl, in her puffy coat and pigtails, was delighted to pet a pack of four-legged

2. See my son's comment back in September about National Talk Like a Pirate Day as evidence of such "infliction."

friends of various shapes and sizes. We got off to a slow start. We should have left our house 20 minutes early.

My middle son galloped ahead with his buddies. All of them were in gym shorts, even though the temperature was near freezing. The dogs looked at them like, "Dude, y'all are crazy."

The older children, including mine, strolled in between those poorly dressed sprinters and the slow-paced canine lovers. They were too cool for this, especially since their parents organized it, yanking them out of bed a good 15 minutes early. Yet, as they walked, they huddled in conversation, sharing secrets about video games and bemoaning Dad jokes. I gave them space, but from a distance, I could tell that they were having fun.

I ambled with my fellow parents. While keeping an eye on the kiddos, we still took in the Halloween decorations of the neighborhood, including the two-story skeleton. As they passed, pedestrians waved, and cars were very willing to let us cross the street. I met some fellow fathers and co-conspirators in this odd and wondrous adventure of parenting. (Your kid also wears shorts when it's freezing outside?!) I even learned a new dad joke: Why did the skeleton not attend the dance? He had no body to go with!

Our kids raced off before they had to endure another joke, slipping through the school doors just before the tardy bell rang.

⁓

I'm all for a walk to school, but I didn't want to take our kids to the roller rink, even though October was National Roller-Skating Month. Imagine that: an entire month dedicated to falling down.

Ginny, however, loves to skate and has accused me of being an old fart.

I thought I had a legitimate alibi: no socks. Ginny pointed out that the rink sold socks. "Yours to keep," the employee smiled. As I grumbled, "Lucky me," I pulled on my own tube socks, laced up my skates, and wobbled onto the rink to Taylor Swift's "Bad Blood."

Our kids had only skated once in their entire lives, which would have been obvious to any outside observer. In fact, there were a dozen or so spectators perched on rickety wooden benches just outside the rink, mostly grandmothers (including my mother-in-law). Both our oldest and youngest children stuck close to the handrail. Better safe than sorry. But the middle child, trying hard to skate on his own, had a couple of sprawling crashes. I tried to help, but the truth is that I only know vague advice like "Bend your knees."[3]

My son wheeled over to his grandmother in the bleachers and sat down in tears. Looking at him, my childhood memories, circa 1989, became as vivid as the sweaty, metallic smell from the handrail. I was back at that friend's birthday party when I crashed, legs splayed, in front of everyone. The cool kids zoomed by, laughing at me. Eventually, I sat alone in the spectator area, fighting back tears.

Ah, so that was the real reason that I didn't want to come to the rink.

I gave my son a few minutes with his grandmother. Then, slowly, I rolled over to him and offered my hand. He shook his head, and I didn't pressure him. I managed to skate another slow lap around the rink. But as I approached the peanut gallery again, I saw him get up and reach for me. Now it was my turn to blink back tears.

Maybe my son will never be a talented skater. Who cares? I hope he remembers that he tried something hard and fell down, but got back up and tried again.

I also get to keep my tube socks.

～

I'm fascinated by collective nouns, which refer to a group of the same type of animal. What an appropriate thing to look up on National Dictionary Day!

---

3. I'm a baseball guy. I don't actually know if "bend your knees" is good advice for roller skating, but in this case, it is certainly preferable to "keep your eye on the ball."

We might call a group of children a pack, a herd, or even a gaggle. A group of kids might climb up and down trees like squirrels in a scurry. Like otters, they are a romp in creeks and streams, not to mention your living room. Granted, children might seem more like rhinos in a crash as they move through your house.

More positively, they are like certain species of big cats: leopards in a leap or hyenas in a cackle.

Kids do have a certain charm, like finches; others exhibit the flamboyance of flamingos. Thinking of more birds, owls gather in parliaments and eagles in convocations. As a Presbyterian, I find it hilarious that a group of vultures is known as a committee. But maybe instead of such an organized and somber gathering, young ones are more likely to convene like parrots—in a pandemonium!

Or maybe in a lounge, like lizards.

Maybe, similar to ferrets, you are unable to comprehend their actions—a fesnyng, whatever that means.

As a parent, I get that it's not all fun and games. I wouldn't normally compare anyone to buffalos, but let's face it—kids can be an obstinacy. Like goldfish, a bunch of them could get into a trouble.

But keep in mind that a swarm of ladybugs is called a loveliness. The other day, a few of my fellow dads and I were watching like a tower of long-necked giraffes as our kids played tag on the other side of the playground fence. They were all scurrying, leaping, and romping with abandon and glee. Call it organized pandemonium. While none of them were wearing a white outfit with black stripes (or a black one with white stripes), I still thought of zebras. Those kids were a dazzle.

⁓

October 28 is Plush Animal Lovers Day. The "stuffies" in our house have been with us from the start. The boys had animal themes as decorations for their nurseries—owls for our firstborn, foxes for his brother. Their collections eventually grew to include other plush animals, including snakes.

Our daughter has taken it to greater heights.

Since the time she could talk, she has wanted to be a tiger. She possesses two stuffed tigers: one named Christmas due to Santa's gift, and another named Frosting due to his white fur. She has a stuffed sea turtle named Broccoli because he is green, and a penguin named Walnut for unknown reasons. Syrup is a hedgehog. Her names extend beyond food—Patch the dog, Sniffles the bear, and Muggie the octopus. My favorite name belongs to her largest stuffy, a round pink cat that she named Great Wall of China.

One of my enduring memories of the COVID-19 pandemic were "stuffy walks," so named because my children would bring along a companion or two for hikes in the neighborhood woods. Shortly before the pandemic, a massive oak had fallen over the neighborhood creek. The kids would splash and jump in the water, and I'd sit on the trunk next to stuffed tigers, lions, and bears.

The other day, I caved and bought a small wolf for her from a toy store. On the drive home, we discussed various names—Gray, Fang, or Wolfie. At a stoplight, I looked in the rearview and caught her smile.

"I know," she said, "let's call him Hope."

November: Master Beginners

On November 1, I attended a service on All Saints Day with a few dozen worshippers scattered among the pews. After scripture readings, the adult choir sang the *Nunc dimittis*, a compline prayer that was especially poignant as the preface to the reading of the names of those who had died in the past year. Each saint was named, and a bell chimed. We came forward and lit candles.

Afterwards, I chitchatted in the narthex. I joked with a few people I knew. A friend told a story that included a few gentle curse words. I shared about hustling down the street, late for this service, when an undergraduate shouted, "Slow down, homie!" Homie? Is that expression, along with Mom jeans, making a comeback?

During the worship service, I remembered a recently deceased woman who liked to say that she had followed her family to North Carolina from Florida only because "Florida got to be too much Florida." She laughed in her hoarse, throaty way.

She grew up in the mountains of northern Nevada. On Sundays, her family would rise before dawn and hike to a little chapel on top of a ridge. I tried to imagine this experience. To be awakened by a gentle yet firm shake. Dress in darkness. Use a lantern to navigate the path ahead, or maybe the bright moon above. Your legs would tire as the climb got steeper, but breathing hard, you would press on and just make it to the summit as the sun crested the mountain range, the first pinks and oranges heralding the resurrection of a new day. As my friend's health declined over the past several months, she returned to this childhood memory. She would say, "I think of that little church in the bare dawn, and it's like I'm there again." She chuckled. "But I don't have to hear a damn sermon."

～

The Earl of Sandwich loved gambling. He loved it so much that he instructed his cook to prepare a meal for him so that he could eat without utensils, preferably with only one hand, in order to gamble with his other. The Earl of Sandwich and his personal attendants had recently been gambling along the Mediterranean Sea, and this cook witnessed a dish prepared by Greek and Turkish chefs. In a hasty facsimile of their culinary creation, he slapped a hunk of meat between two slices of bread and served it to his lord.

Sandwich is a town near the eastern coast of England, but in America, the sandwich became associated with the working class. During the Great Depression, a restaurant in New Orleans pledged to feed striking streetcar workers for free. Before opening their diner, Benny and Clovis Martin had worked in that industry under poor conditions. To feed the strikers, they fried seafood, which was readily available in the Gulf of Mexico, and stuck it between slices of French bread. Benny later claimed that, whenever he saw a striker enter the diner, he'd shout to his brother, "Here comes another poor boy!" New Orleans is famous for the Po' Boy today, and other parts of the country have copied it.

"Poor boy" might seem paternalistic. It certainly would be in certain contexts. But the Martin brothers were former streetcar workers. They provided free food for the striking workers and intended "Po' Boy" as an expression of solidarity. It reminds me of the earliest followers of Jesus, who pooled their resources. They broke bread together to ensure that no one in their community would go without food. Jesus had requested that this act of communion serve as a memorial to him. Food doesn't have to be fancy to be holy.

While National Sandwich Day is November 3 to mark the Earl of Sandwich's birthday, the Martins's spirit of sharing is more like the teachings of Christ, who said that the last shall be first and the first shall be last. And that whoever wished to be the greatest would become the servant of all.

~

Parents know that the real zombies are not out on Halloween, but a few mornings after another yearly event—the End of Daylight Savings Time. Cue a witch's cackle and the piping of a ghoulish organ. A young child's sleep schedule is sacred, and this fiendish disruption will haunt parents for days, if not weeks.

I know that we "fall back" and, in theory, gain an extra hour. But the clocks change at some forsaken, vampire hour early Sunday morning. Children do not sleep in. Kids are up early and, come bedtime, are not ready to sleep, meaning they stay up later. On Monday morning, cue the grumpy zombies.

Why do we subject ourselves to such torture? Something to do with farming? Do farmers actually care?

If the powers that be wish to continue this practice, I have a compromise. Better yet, an opportunity. Set the clock back an hour to 9:00 p.m. on the first Friday in November. Ginny and I will get a babysitter. There's a possibility I might even make it into dessert without turning it into a pumpkin.

~

You remember Ramona (see National Dog Appreciation Day in August). Our family's house coyote has a taste for stuffed animals (see National Plush Animal Appreciation Day in October). Ramona first chews off the plastic eyes before methodically de-stuffing the toy in a cloud of cotton. I'm fine with thinning out the herd of stuffies. But occasionally, she gets a hold of one of the upper echelon of animals that cuddle with a child at bedtime. We seek Nana's assistance when one of these items sustains damage. She not only restuffs and sews the plush animal back together; she also replaces the eyes and nose with buttons.

National Button Day is November 16, which this year falls on the third Thursday of November. I assume you don't highlight this little holiday on your calendar like you do the following week. Buttons are indeed small. They fit between two fingers. Their size contributes to their usefulness, as even a child can easily manipulate them. However, buttons are strong enough to keep together a shirt or hold up a pair of pants. As I write, I'm wearing a flannel shirt with mahogany brown buttons. Stitching through four holes holds them in place. My jeans have a bronze-colored button. A metal tab secures it to the denim. The same basic design from the thirteenth century served as the foundation for these clever innovations.

You can find buttons in every color and shape. They may shine or sparkle. Modern clothes often feature fake pockets with a sewn-shut hole, indicating the button's decorative or ornamental nature. Buttons are beautiful! Both young and young at heart use buttons for art. If a dog chews up a stuffed animal, buttons can be the eyes and nose.

Nana, like her mom, her grandmother, and her great-grandmother, for whom she was named, keeps a glass container full of discarded or previously abandoned buttons. When I was growing up, Mom would dig into this jar not for stuffed animal repair but whenever someone popped a button, say, playing backyard football. This saved money. There is no sense in buying a new pair of jeans when you can repair the ones you own.

I also remember that these slightly mismatched buttons gave me pause. Perhaps there were times when I was a little embarrassed. But mostly, the button caused me to remember the person who sewed it. I hope that sometimes I even thanked her. Any practice of gratitude begins with stopping to pay attention.

◦≈◦

This year, I wished to start a Thanksgiving tradition: a family football game. *Touch* football, mind you; I like my relatives and wish no bodily harm. I did, however, want my nuclear family to win.

I prepped my own kids with a few passing plays. Nothing complicated. Simple routes like the slant and the buttonhook.[1] One of their favorite plays was The Bomb. They were to run as fast as possible, and I would throw for a touchdown.

While our relatives were receptive to the initial idea, other tasks took precedent that early afternoon, including preparations for the feast. I won't argue with that. When the time came for kick-off, the only available players were eleven years old and younger. Still, I was game. The other adults appreciated that I had the hungry kids out of the kitchen.

We suffered a delay, however, when the cousins argued about picking teams. Finally, we believed we had resolved the conflict, but my daughter had a change of heart. This sparked a more furious debate. My younger son, the middle child and often the peacemaker, piped up, "Why don't we all run the bomb and see who can catch the ball?"

I shouted, "Hike!" After they took off, I lobbed the Nerf ball into the crisp air. My oldest almost snagged it, but it bounced off his hands and rolled crazily across the grass. They all raced after it and piled on top of each other. A cousin emerged from the scrum, holding the ball aloft. My daughter was thrilled for him: "Touchup!" Her brothers tried to explain that the term was *touchdown*. She remained adamant; her cousin was holding the ball up.

---

1. Also known as the comeback pattern, a receiver runs forward, then turns and runs a few steps back toward the quarterback. On the heels of National Button Day, I note that the buttonhook refers to a tool shaped in this running pattern that is used to pull a button through the hole and fasten it. A button hook is a helpful device and unique among the destructive, violent language of football; for example, see The Bomb. Also, Louis Jenkins has a delightful wordplay in a poem "Football" in which the narrator takes a "snap," referring to the quarterback receiving the ball at the start of a football play, only to realize this "snap" is something entirely different: "What the hell is this? 'This isn't a football; it's a shoe, a man's brown leather oxford." I love this poem. You can find it on the Poetry Foundation's website.

All of this excitement drew the attention of the house coyote, who had been dozing in the sunshine beside the back steps. After the kids lined up again and took off for another bomb, Ramona streaked like a wide receiver. She beat them to the bouncing ball and picked it up in her teeth. Ramona raced all over the yard, weaving in and out of laughing children, avoiding their gleeful tackling attempts. Eventually, the kids were scattered across the lawn on their backs, breathless with effort, and Ramona triumphantly chewed the corner of the Nerf ball like a stogie.

~

My middle child has been in the tae kwon do program for two years. I've witnessed dozens of students break a board for the first time. After just the second lesson, the instructor summons the new student, typically from lower elementary school, to the front of the class, where he splits a slender piece of wood with a downward chop of his fist, to the cheers of the other students. The instructors hold the board in such a way that you really can't miss it.[2] After the board break, the instructor gets down on one knee and ties the white belt around the student's waist. Then the student scampers happily back to the group. It's a genius marketing move on the part of the instructors; the experience makes them want to continue in tae kwon do and break more boards with increasingly difficult punches and kicks.

This particular day, a young child came up to the front of the class for their first board break. They smashed the wood into two pieces with their fist, and everyone applauded. The teacher instructed the child to extend their arms so he could tie their

2. The fact that the student can't miss the board reminds me of cutting the umbilical cord for my children, and how the doctor handed over the scissors only after the nurses had positioned everything perfectly and left the slightest opening to make the cut. Now that I'm thinking about it, I'm wondering if giving the non-birthing partner a role actually encourages them to have more children, just as letting a novice break a board typically encourages them to continue in tae kwon do. However, one should exercise caution when applying this metaphor too broadly.

belt. They spread their arms like a bird's wings. Only they flew in and hugged the instructor!

This child desired human contact, not mere material awards. They celebrated by reaching for a relationship. The student had become the master.

December: Good Hmphfs

ONCE UPON A TIME, I was absolutely convinced that no parent should willfully deceive a child with an elaborate fairy tale about a jolly old man in a sleigh pulled by a flying reindeer. While people move past the Santa myth, I argued that too many adults cling to harmful fantasies.

Ginny suggested that perhaps I should wait to make up my mind about such stories until we actually had children.

About four years later, our three-year-old son lay in bed on Christmas Eve. He wondered: How do reindeer fly? How does Santa carry all those presents? How does Santa make it all the way around the world in one night? And what about kids, like his best friend from preschool, whose homes don't have chimneys? How does Santa bring his gifts inside?

I lay there in the dark, trying to think of something to say.

Finally, my son sighed, "Daddy, it's *such* a good story."

～

On December 4, National Sock Day reminded me of a mentor who worked as a chaplain for the hospital's pediatric oncology unit. On the first day of orientation for the new pastoral students, he warned us, "Don't you dare refer to our patients as 'cancer kids.'" Later that morning, mirth shone from his eyes as he showed us his socks. One was bright pink, and the other was neon yellow.

Over the course of my studies, I learned that he had more bright colors, like lime green and royal purple, and that he would often mix-and-match. Other socks had funky geometric designs. Still others had pictures of wacky cartoon animals: toucans, sloths, zebras, and snails. He wore socks depicting our solar system's planets, the Paris skyline, and pepperoni pizza slices. In terms of sock selection, he had only one rule: no clowns. "Some kids are afraid of them," he said, before adding with a wink, "some adults, too."

His silly socks served a very serious purpose. "It gives you something to talk about when there's really nothing that can be said."

This chaplain has died, but he felt very present just the other day in my office. A grieving father sat across from me. Through his tears, he pointed to my taco socks. I wiped my own eyes and said softly, "It's Tuesday, after all."

He cracked a smile, and then a giggle spilled from his lips. We cried some more.

I certainly don't have answers to tragedies, like why some kids are so sick, but I always remember the last day of my education at the hospital. As he addressed us, my mentor wore socks adorned with those funny-looking, four-cornered graduation caps. "Do random acts of kindness for someone you don't even know. And if you really love someone, tell them so while you can in this life."

～

My buddy Walter was suffering from COVID for the second time. He was achy and fatigued, but he still had his marvelous sense of humor. So, he wrote to me on Saint Nicholas Day (December 6) that his six-year-old had asked what the difference was between Saint Nick and Santa Claus. Through his fog, Walter replied, "Well, Saint Nicholas was a real person... I mean, um, what were we talking about?"

I told him about the hot topic in my household: What do Santa's reindeer eat?

On one side of the debate, my oldest child maintains that reindeer eat corn and carrots, preferably with the green stems still on top. He cites internet research on the habits of reindeer. But my youngest counters that magical flying reindeer eat *candy* corn and carrot *cake*. All creatures residing at the North Pole consume sweets, as everyone knows.

As is often the case, the tiebreaker fell to the middle child. After weighing the options, he renders this verdict: Give the vegetables to the reindeer and the candy to the kids.

~

"Our daughter still hums as she eats her breakfast cereal."

My friend Meg wrote this memorable line in a Christmas letter six years ago. I've hung on to it, for I delight in the poetry of her words and how the image resonates with my own son—not that he hums or eats cereal. He has a similar daydreaming quality.

In today's world of social media, the Christmas letter is becoming yet another relic of the past. Why take the time to inform friends and loved ones about your lives when they can see for themselves on Facebook and Instagram? I appreciate those updates throughout the year, whether it's pictures from the first day of school, a post about a child's soccer goal, or the obituary of a grandparent.

But, without sounding hopelessly outdated, isn't there still a place for the Christmas letter?

National Christmas Card Day (December 9) is a time for sitting down and writing about the past year's accomplishments, disappointments, struggles, and graces. A Christmas letter is like a piece of poetry to me. Not that it has to rhyme, but as W.H. Auden wrote, "Poetry makes nothing happen." Is this a comment on the futility of language to affect the world around us? Or, as Ross Gay has argued, the point may be that "nothing" can actually happen—a halt on so-called production and output.[1] By

1. Gay, 44

conveying insight and emotion into our intimate lives, Christmas letters invite us to slow down.

When someone asks how I am doing, I often reply, "Busy." The person nods, understanding that being busy is the expected response. But a poem is a daydream, a hum, a faraway look. Taking the time to write and send a Christmas letter is nothing like our face-paced world. Therefore, such things can mean something special. Where else am I going to get a glimpse of a child humming over her cereal bowl?

My youngest is now six years old. Just recently, she came home with a piece of paper where she'd written that the "best part of me" were her ears because "they help me to hear birds."

～

December 21 is the longest night of the year. Our culture primarily views light as positive and good, while viewing darkness as negative, even evil. But the longest night or winter solstice is a cause for celebration. This holiday has ancient roots in many cultures. Today, people still exchange gifts and feast with family and friends.

Before dawn, I snuggled with the house coyote on our couch, sipping coffee as the rest of my family slept. I heard the recycling truck rumble in the alley. My companion remained asleep; so much for being a watchdog.

Generally, I take for granted the activities that people engage in during the night. The food that is delivered. The roads that are repaired. The buildings that are cleaned. I understand that human effort, not magic, removes my garbage, but it's only when these things fail that I become conscious of them. Then, I find myself grumbling and complaining like a tired machine. Or a scrooge.

December 21 is also National Humbug Day. Like Ebeneezer Scrooge, one can vent frustrations, "Bah, humbug!" Not everything is merry and bright.

While my dog slumbered, my thoughts rolled toward those who toiled through the night. It's not just the sanitation workers, but also the police, cleaning crews, and hospital workers. In a patient's room, I have witnessed people lifting their groans and prayers into the liminal space between hope and reality. I have witnessed people doing what they can—changing a bandage, adjusting the bed sheets, or holding a cool compress against the skin slick with sweat.

My church, like many others, offers a Longest Night service to make space for what Saint John of the Cross referred to as dark nights of the soul—anxiety, suffering, and grief. There may not be answers or explanations, but we can gather together for support as we await the coming dawn. Sometimes a single lit candle means the most. Sometimes, it's just one person.

The writer Brian Doyle was a friend of mine who died much too young. He was known for making contented grunts whenever something pleased him—a noise that David James Duncan described as Mama Goat Hmphfs, perhaps because our buddy was also a hirsute fellow.[2] I enjoyed thinking of Brian sounding like a mama nuzzling her kids. This time of year, I often remember him because he loved the magic of Christmas. He would chortle, recalling my firstborn's words, "It is such a good story."

On December 21, the sun came up. I got off the couch to run an errand at a certain warehouse-type store, which was one of the last places I wished to be on God's green Earth, enclosed by granite, navigating gaudy holiday wares and exhausted employees, with everything bathed in a hellish glow of overhead fluorescent light. Bah, humbug.

Over by the shiny red display of Christmas cards was a goateed gentleman, probably in his sixties. His hair was gray and thinning, and his clothes were a little rumpled. Nothing unusual or striking would stop you, especially if you were trying to buy batteries for your kid's gift and get the heck out of there.

I just happened to hear him open a card, read the inside, and then carefully return it to its rightful place.

He was making the Mama Goat Hmphfs.

---

2. Duncan in the Foreword (Doyle, xvi)

Brian once prayed, "We are part of a Mystery we cannot understand, and we are grateful."[3]

~

In the last week of the year, one might reflect on the highs and lows of 2023 or make resolutions for the future. At the end of a book, one might sit quietly and reflect on the various national days as a way to summarize lessons learned. These lessons and themes include the possibility of joy amid grief, the awareness and cultivation of gratitude, the courage to become vulnerable, and the miracle of grace under duress.

One might also have one's hands full of the endless tasks of taking care of young children at home during school break.

I was thus engaged with scrubbing the breakfast pans when my three kids began to discuss heaven at our humble kitchen table. They imagined eating all their favorite foods: candy, donuts, and Al's Burgers, a Chapel Hill restaurant that is award-winning in this life and, apparently, the one beyond. After indulging in their favorite foods, they envisioned endless gaming sessions.

Then the youngest exclaimed that, in heaven, she could finally meet her namesake, her maternal great-great-grandmother. This matriarch of my wife's family had already died before I entered the picture. Her family lovingly remembered her as someone who did not tolerate foolishness. The description of her reminds me of Ms. Ann, my former parishioner. (Remember Ms. Ann from May? Maybe I should also write a limerick about Mama Sadie.) Even so, my wife recalls this matriarch furnishing aluminum pie pans for the grandchildren's backyard game of mud kitchen. It is an image of playfulness and grace.

Back at our messy table, my sons told their younger sister that not only would she meet her namesake but also many other relatives, even people whose names we didn't know. Even our caveman relatives!

3. Doyle, 197

No one knows exactly what heaven is like. But even stuck in the mess and muddle of a day's chores, one can contemplate how we are connected to the past and future through the mystery of love. As another mystic sage once wrote, "For now we see through a glass, darkly; now I know in part; but then shall I know even as I am also known."[4] I have my children to thank for that reminder.

I also asked them to bring their dirty plates to the sink. They weren't going to clean themselves.

∼

Wrapping up the year, my young family and I relaxed post-Christmas with a few days at the beach. Back home in Chapel Hill, I often joke with my kids that, if they are really as bored as they say, they can go jump in the neighborhood pool.

But swim in the ocean?! They didn't think I was actually serious until they saw their mother putting on her bathing suit.

These so-called polar plunges—when people jump into icy water or run into the freezing ocean to raise money for charity—most often take place on the first day of the new year. But we had to get home before New Year's Day. These events draw big crowds, but because we were early, I expected that my family would be the only ones on the beach.

As we descended the stairs at the public access, there was a lone woman walking her dog. The wind whipped up, and I saw her pull her heavy coat more tightly around her. I also saw her jaw drop when she noticed that we were taking off our jackets to reveal our swimsuits.

Ginny gave her phone to this stranger to video our plunge. We took off running down the beach, yelling until we hit the waves. The freezing water took our breaths away. We splashed around a

---

4. I know that 1 Corinthians 13 is often read at weddings. No offense to you if this beautiful passage was read during your ceremony. The Apostle Paul, however, uses the word agape for love, not eros (romantic love). Agape is the self-sacrificing love that marks parenthood. When Jesus spoke of "the outer darkness with weeping and gnashing of teeth," he was referring to middle school.

bit to make it count, then charged back out to the sand. Our new friend asked my youngest daughter, "How did it feel?"

Through chattering teeth, my girl groaned, "This was Dad's idea."

Fair enough. This year's observation of these eccentric national days has brought its share of revelations and epiphanies, as well as some stress for my family. I'm grateful that they often roll with my ideas. This is especially true when my ideas place them in the icy ocean.

To recall my conversations with Sarah about morning pancakes and Walter about Christmas myths, what will my kids remember? More importantly, what will they remember about me? I hope for my sense of humor. Most of all, I want my family to remember that I loved them fiercely. Although I've paid attention to certain days and what they celebrate, here at the end of this journey, I take the most satisfaction in knowing that I have said "I love you" to each of them every single day.

Properly bundled back on the beach, everyone grinned for a family selfie. Who cares that it wasn't an official holiday? We took the polar plunge! It is *such* a good story.

Appendix A: Calendar of National Days

January 7: Bobblehead Doll Day

January 9: Word Nerd Day

January 19: Tenderness Toward Existence Day

January 25: St. Dwynwen's Day/Cwtch Day

January 28: LEGO Day

February 2: Ukulele Day

February 4: Mail Carrier Appreciation Day

February 8: Preacher's Kid Appreciation Day

February 18: Eat Ice Cream for Breakfast Day

March 14: Chicken Dance Day *Actually, May 14

March 19: Let's Laugh Day

March 21: Teenager Day

March 26: Make Up Your Own Day

April 7: Beer Day

April 10: Encourage a Young Author Day

Last Friday in April: Hairball Awareness Day

April 17: Haiku Day

April 25: Hairdresser Appreciation Day

May 4: Star Wars Day

May 12: Limerick Day

May 14: No-Complaining Day

May 24: Brothers Day

First Friday in June: Donut Day

June 6: Yo-Yo Day

July 2: I Forgot Day

July 6: Fried Chicken Day

Second Friday in July: Motorcycle Day

July 17: Tattoo Day

July 19: Flitch Day

July 24: Cousins Day

First Saturday in August:
Disc Golf Day

August 8: Pickleball Day

August 12: Middle Child Day

August 18: Serendipity Day

August 26: Dog
Appreciation Day

September 2: Hummingbird Day

September 5: Beard Day

Second Tuesday in September:
Ants on a Log Day

September 8: Ampersand Day

September 13: Positive
Thinking Day

September 19: Talk Like a
Pirate Day

September 21: Miniature
Golf Day

September 24: Bluebird
of Happiness Day

September 26: Johnny
Appleseed Day

October: Pumpkin Spice month

October: Roller-Skating month

October 6: Garlic Lovers Day

First Wednesday in October:
Walk to School Day

October 16: Dictionary Day

October 28: Plush Animal
Lovers Day

November 3: Sandwich Day

November 16: Button Day

December 4: Sock Day

December 9: Christmas
Card Writing Day

December 21: Humbug Day

Appendix B: Alphabetical List of National Days

Ampersand Day

Ants on a Log Day

Beard Day

Beer Day

Bluebird of Happiness Day

Bobblehead Doll Day

Brothers Day

Button Day

Chicken Dance Day

Christmas Card Writing Day

Cousins Day

Dictionary Day

Disc Golf Day

Dog Appreciation Day

Donut Day

Eat Ice Cream for Breakfast Day

Encourage a Young Author Day

Flitch Day

Fried Chicken Day

Garlic Lovers Day

Haiku Day

Hairball Awareness Day

Hairdresser Appreciation Day

Humbug Day

Hummingbird Day

I Forgot Day

Johnny Appleseed Day

LEGO Day

Let's Laugh Day

Limerick Day

Mail Carrier Appreciation Day

Make Up Your Own Day

Middle Child Day

Miniature Golf Day

Motorcycle Day

No-Complaining Day

Pickleball Day

Plush Animal Lovers Day

Positive Thinking Day

Preacher's Kid Appreciation Day

Sandwich Day

Serendipity Day

Sock Day

St. Dwynwen's Day/Cwtch Day

Star Wars Day

Talk Like a Pirate Day

Tattoo Day

Teenager Day

Tenderness Toward Existence Day

Ukulele Day

Walk to School Day

Word Nerd Day

Yo-Yo Day

Bibliography

Doyle, Brian. *One Long River of Song: Notes on Wonder*. New York: Little, Brown and Company, 2020.

Gay, Ross. *Inciting Joy: Essays*. Chapel Hill, NC: Algonquin, 2022.

———. *Against Which: Poems*. Fort Lee, NJ: Cavan Kerry, 2006.

Grace, Annie. *This Naked Mind: Control Alcohol, Find Freedom, Discover Happiness & Change Your Life*. New York: Avery, 2018.

Hirschfield, Jane. *Ten Windows: How Great Poems Change the World*. New York: Knopf, 2017.

King, Martin Luther Jr. *Strength to Love*. Philadelphia: Fortress, 1963.

For more information on the national days referenced in this book (as well as thousands more), visit NationalToday.com and NationalDayCalendar. com. Have fun!

"Andrew's wordy nerdy joy (he was born on National Word Nerd Day, after all) pulled me into each month's essay; his childlike sense of wonder and his deep orientation toward love for those around him brought me along as a participant in his experiments to find the sublime in the ordinary. This is a great read for anyone seeking words of tenderness and delight."

—John Walter Fitchett Canter Jr., pastor and word writer

"With a minister's heart and a writer's eye, Taylor-Troutman here chronicles revelation in a thousand everyday turns and relationships during the course of a year's unofficial holidays. He invites his readers into nothing less than 'entangled joy,' joy not contingent on the absence of suffering and loss, but joy that 'emerges from how we care for each other through those things . . .' His invitation is timely, courageous, convincing, and beautiful."

—E. Carson Brisson, emeritus associate professor of Bible & biblical languages, Union Presbyterian Seminary

"This book! A tour of unofficial national holidays, *This IS the Day* is a party-hatted feast of fun and a tonic of tenderness. Taylor-Troutman is a trustworthy guide. He leads with love. As a partner, parent, and pastor he revels in the 'pied beauty' of this life. With a wonder that is often scrubbed from grown-up sensibility, he keeps pointing, keeps calling us to look and see. And, yes—rejoice!"

—Andrew Nagy-Benson, senior pastor, The Congregational Church of Middlebury

"By paying attention to the places where his own daily life intersects with obscure national observances of peculiar things and strange events, Andrew Taylor-Troutman maps for us a day-by-day journey filled with tender delights and entangled joys. Seeking the extraordinary within the ordinary (and the ordinary within the extraordinary), *This IS the Day* provides a seriously fun (and well-footnoted! and enthusiastic!) accompaniment for us as we make another trip around the sun. What a joy to read!"

—Shan Overton, dean of academics, American Baptist College